THE SERENITY CODE

A PERSONAL JOURNEY TO WELLNESS

LOUISE CLAIRE-PARDOE
& JASON PAUL CLAIRE

The Serenity Code

A personal journey to wellness

©Louise Claire-Pardoe and Jason Paul Claire

ISBN: 978-1-906316-71-6

Published in 2010 by HotHive Books, Evesham, UK.
www.thehothive.com

A CIP record of this book is available from the British Library.

Printed in the UK by TJ International, Padstow.

The authors of this book do not dispense medical advice or prescribe the use of any technique as a form of treatment for physical, emotional or medical problems without the advice of a doctor, either directly or indirectly. The intent of the authors is only to offer information of a general nature to help you in your quest for emotional and spiritual wellness.

With heartfelt gratitude this book is dedicated to
Source; the all-giving, loving and silent watcher at the centre of everything.
Gaia for nurturing us and providing us with so much beauty.
Our families who gave us life, supported and encouraged us.
Our friends for always believing in us.
Each other; best friends, life partners, twin flames.
And to Pringle, for just being Pringle.

ACKNOWLEDGEMENTS

So much has happened in our lives up to this point. Both of us have undergone amazing experiences that have led us to where we are right now on our journey. Along our path we have had the great privilege of learning from many teachers.

These teachers have come in all shapes and sizes, from all walks of life, including all of our family and friends, and each being that we have ever connected with in the physical and etheric worlds. We give thanks in particular to all beings of light, and the silent watcher ever present at the centre of consciousness.

We thank each and every one who has touched our world, past, present and future, and wish you love and happiness always.

TABLE OF CONTENTS

When we first started on our own path of self development over 10 years ago, we couldn't have been more sceptical about the field of personal development. Firmly locked into our left-brain, physical world, all the decisions that we made came from a place of fear and, as a result, we were suffering from ill-health and poor family relationships. Our world wasn't working for us, and we desperately needed to change. Ten years later, our world is unrecognisable; full of health, peace and joy. What follows is our story, which we hope will inspire and motivate you to challenge your beliefs and view of the world and, in so doing, rediscover your own innate ability to live a life abundant with health and wellness.

Artwork

All the artwork in this book is original and created by Jason who has been drawing for the whole of his life. After being diagnosed with severe depression as a result of workplace bullying, he spent hours sitting and drawing in order to help him recover and progress towards his own health and wellness. As a result, he discovered that his art had a powerful healing effect. The art came directly from Jason's heart and soul, allowing him the space to express deeply buried emotions and release them from his energy field. Over time, Jason recovered to full health and is now inspired to create drawings that speak to the hearts and souls of others, enabling them to develop and heal on deep levels.

You will find a piece of Jason's artwork at the beginning of each chapter. Each drawing is imbued with powerful healing energy. It is recommended that before and after each chapter, you spend 5 minutes gently focusing on the art and the affirmation underneath to allow energetic changes to occur within your energy field. This will prepare you for the chapter ahead, thus facilitating your journey.

Step stone wisdom

You will notice that each chapter has been called a 'step stone'. The reason for this is to break down your development journey into manageable stages. Move at your own pace through each of the step stones, ensuring that you are comfortable with the information provided within each one before you move on. Remember that the artwork will also support you on your journey, so spend time with Jason's drawings before and after each step stone. Follow your inner guidance and progress through the book at a pace that is exactly right for you.

Activities and reflections

Throughout the book there are gentle activities and moments for reflection to help support your journey. Moments for reflection are indicated by a box illustrated with a swan; activities are indicated by a box illustrated with flowers. Please take the time to work through each of the activities and reflections provided, making notes as appropriate, to develop a deeper connection to yourself and others and move onwards towards health and wellness.

And finally…
By following this book in the manner indicated you will make significant changes in your world, just as we have changed our own. We wish you health and happiness on your journey.

Blessings

Louise

Louise and Jason

All artwork in this book is available in full colour as a print, card or bookmark. See useful contacts at the end of the book for more information.

'A mind all logic is like a knife all blade. It makes the hand bleed that uses it.'

Rabindranath Tagore

We do not enter into this life with a guidebook. From our very first breath we slowly learn how to experience the world we perceive around us. Regardless of where in the world we are born, who our parents are, what culture or religion we are born into, over time we find our own way of being in the world, our own way of understanding and viewing the world. No one else will ever experience the world in the way that we do. We begin life full of infinite potential, limitless possibilities.

Physical life is relatively simple; to undergo experiences and to live life, as much as we are able, in health and wellness. Along this journey that we call life, we find our own way. For the vast majority of us there are parts of the journey that are extremely challenging, that cause us great pain and upset. How we deal with these parts of the journey in that moment, and in the days, months and years that follow, are the key to our wellness.

It is important to understand that on the journey of life we do have choices in the face of what life throws our way. As the Buddha said 'No one outside of ourselves can rule us inwardly'. In other words, we have a choice over how we react to external influences around us that we may not be able to control. One way guarantees our wellness, the other does not.

Standing at the crossroads of any challenge, we have the power to choose one of two ways: the path of love and acceptance, or the path of fear and struggle. In the Western world this concept may seem totally alien because over a period of many years, as a culture, we have succeeded in giving our power away. Giving away responsibility for everything that happens in our life, to the point where we look for answers outside of ourselves as opposed to within. As a result of this, we may feel powerless in times of crisis, believing that we do not have the tools or understanding to deal healthfully and mindfully with what life throws across our path. Holding the belief that we do not have a choice means that we have totally disconnected from the truth of life and our birthright, and our wellness suffers.

Our birthright is health, happiness and wellness. These are created when we are 'in the flow' and as a result of the choices that we make to enable us to cope peacefully with daily life. Unfortunately, modern day childhood deconstructs the power and beauty of our minds, which understand this concept, and most of us learn to disconnect from the interconnectedness and the flow all around us. This creates a world of separation and fear, cloaking the reality that everything in existence is intimately and perfectly connected in Oneness. Let's look at nature; everything in nature is perfectly and inherently linked. Life is generally easier when we flow, like a droplet of water negotiating calm streams or swift rapids, it does not resist and is taken exactly where it needs to be, following its natural course. The droplet of water doesn't fear the path that it is taking, even though its journey may be challenging at times. It merely accepts its journey, never resisting.

Nature never disconnects from itself, and while nature can be cruel, what we have to realise is that this is part of the flow, of the oneness and interdependency of everything around it. Human beings, on the other hand, have learnt to be fearful of living in the flow. Ignoring natural laws, we worry about what might be and 'What if?' This simple action creates resistance, instantly disconnecting us from the flow, subsequently making life more challenging. There are merely two states in the human psyche: one is fear, and the other is love. When we learn to live in the flow and reconnect to the natural laws, we are able to create from a space of love and acceptance. While the going may be tough, we choose to accept the flow and create peace, leading onward to a state of wellness. When we make a choice out of fear, we resist the natural flow in that given moment, disconnecting us and creating resistance, which our bodies feel as stress or anxiety.

The key to reconnection and moving onwards to health and wellness is realising that we cannot stop the flow of life, and that we merely have choices as to how we react while in the flow. We can react through the heart, which is our seat of personal power, love and acceptance, or through the head, which is renowned for its fear-based decisions.

One cannot exist without the other so, for optimal results, both head and heart should be working equally and in tandem, to support us through the inherent ebbs and flows of life in a more instinctive way, rather than having an imbalance of one or the other. When the head and the heart work against these natural laws of balance disconnection is created, producing feelings of anxiety, anger and fear about what life may hold for us. We may feel powerless and unable to control anything around us. Yet you always have choices when you are in the flow. Even when you think you don't have a choice, you have made the choice not to have the choice!

The irony of this whole scenario is that our natural state of being is one of wellness and infinite potential. However, because of our life journey and the influences and beliefs acquired along the way, many of us choose to create a reality of fear, hardship and struggle. Inner peace and wellness are merely a choice away, if you just allow yourself to see the world in a different way, to realise that you cannot control life and its flow, but that a change in your perspective about how you view it is all that is needed. This knowledge is your birthright.

We used to live in a world that was full of fear and anxiety because of the choices that we made. Our world was home to serious health conditions, work-related stress, poor family relations and an overwhelming feeling of fear and dread. Over the past 10 years we have taken a life-changing journey deep inside ourselves, with the support of some amazing mentors, books and therapy, and chosen a new direction for our lives; choosing the pathway of health, happiness and wellness. Everything we write in this book comes directly from our hearts, in absolute truth. We have been right to the very bottom of the pit of fear and despair, yet we found a way out. We wish to share these stepping stones with you, in the hope that you might be inspired to take a new road for your journey in life; one which leads you directly to wellness.

Why not make a conscious choice, right now, to release that which is holding you back or causing you fear, worry or anxiety. The only way to change a situation or to experience release is to take action and try out something different. Perhaps this book will be part of your journey. Allowing yourself to do this will not only reconnect you to that which you were never actually disconnected from, but in so doing help you to rediscover wellness; assisting you to deepen and improve all relationships within your life, most importantly within yourself. From this point on, know that you always have choices every second of your life and that you are the master of your own destiny. You may have spent your whole life believing that you are not in control. While you may not be able to control what life hands you, you are able to control your choices and how you react to the situations you find yourself in. Embark on this journey and take steps to free yourself from the bar-less prison that you may find yourself in. It is so powerfully destructive to put yourself into a box, so are you now ready to achieve your full potential?

In this book we share with you our personal healing journey, step stone by step stone, providing you with our exercises and thoughts, based on our experiences over the past decade and beyond. Therefore, please take what feels instinctively right for you and leave to one side what doesn't. We all have a different view of the world and the understanding presented here is a work in progress of years of personal experience. Designed as a supportive tool, we have written this book to inspire and motivate you to make changes in your life, if that is what you wish for. May health, happiness and wellness fill all the days of your life.

'Love is the only reality and it is not a mere sentiment. It is the ultimate truth that lies at the heart of creation.'

Rabindranath Tagore

Like most people, we have both been on a long, transformative journey in life, taking us through a multitude of highs and lows. Our journey has shaped us and made us who we are today; our thoughts, actions, beliefs and health are a direct result of the experiences that we have undergone. We wish to share our stories with you, to show that from deeply dark and difficult times, it is possible to make lasting changes and to rediscover health, happiness and wellness simply through the choices that we make. We wish to say a big 'thank you' to everyone and every experience that has featured in our lives and for the gifts that they brought and continue to bring. We realise that everyone, including those who feature in our own stories, are on their own personal journey, trying hard to get it 'right'. We impact others just as much as others have impacted us. For this reason we share our story with no judgement or apportionment of blame, for without those experiences we wouldn't be the people we are today, and neither would you.

Louise's story

For the first 30 years of my life, I was a reluctant participant in my earthly incarnation. A quiet baby, I am told that I spent a lot of time asleep, and continue to love sleeping to this day. It is not unusual for me to sleep for 12, sometimes 14, hours at a stretch. I now know that being asleep was my way of escaping the physical world, retreating into a safe world where I didn't have to be 'present'.

I can only remember snippets of my early years: my first ballet lesson (which I hated), my first pony riding lesson (which I quite liked), Christmas and special occasions spent with my grandparents. My happiest memories are of time spent with my grandparents at their caravan at the foot of the Malvern Hills.

I was a painfully shy child and never wanted to do anything that 'normal' children do. My parents would wonder why I wasn't like other children, but I didn't want to be like all the other children; that just wasn't me. I enjoyed my own company, my imaginary friends and my toys, playing within my own world and finding much safety and comfort there. Until I went to school, life was pretty idyllic.

I spent my first day at school underneath my desk not wanting to come out. What on earth had happened to me? Why was I here? I didn't want to be playing with other children; I wanted to be at home playing on my own. I remember distinctly an Australian exchange teacher in my reception class, singling me out at every opportunity. She saw that I was quiet and painfully shy, and was probably trying out some sort of new-fangled 1970s teaching technique to help me to 'come out of my shell'. For years afterwards I carried around a ball of hate and contempt for that woman who would force me to speak up in front of my fellow classmates in every lesson without fail.

The very thought of drawing attention to myself, every eye looking at me, filled me with fear and dread that paralysed every part of my being. I would make myself sick with fear, my stomach would knot up, my chest would tighten and my throat felt as if it was clamped shut. It was the worst feeling imaginable. However, in order to please my parents and to try and ensure that my teacher stopped shouting at me and picking on me, I forced myself to come out of my shell. It wasn't easy. I remember feeling permanently worried and anxious on the inside, but I would never show it on the outside. I still didn't like 'performing' in front of others, but gradually got used to it. Thankfully I did, because if I hadn't overcome this crippling shyness I wouldn't now be able to stand up in front of large auditoriums of people and speak to them.

The rest of my school years passed by with little incident and I grew to love school and my fellow classmates. I nurtured some beautiful and lasting friendships, which continue to this very day, and which I am so grateful for. Middle school and high school throughout the 1980s were the best years of my life. I wasn't an aesthetically pleasing child, so in order to fit in with the popular kids I became the class joker. Most days I would return home with my face aching so much from laughing.

While my school years from the age of nine onwards were very happy, home life was difficult.

During my teens, I found what was to become my vocation. I discovered a natural ability to counsel; to listen to people's worries and concerns and offer neutral, impartial advice. Back then my 'clients' were my mother, my sister and my friends, and I remember this being the beginning of a lifetime of offering support and guidance, listening while they shared with me things that were upsetting to them. I didn't know it then, but I had a very old head on young shoulders.

These experiences laid down solid foundations for my current role in life as a therapist, coach, career consultant and spiritual mentor. I also practised these natural skills with everyone else I met, offering impartial, unbiased support and advice, and as a result, I developed an even larger circle of friends.

Following my GCSEs, I worked as hard as I could for my A levels, knowing that they were my passport to freedom. I was 18 years old and had applied for a degree that included an industrial placement to help me gain work experience. In the summer of 1990, I had a provisional place at university to study European business and I couldn't wait to start.

In August 1990, a group of my friends decided to hire a cottage in the Brecon Beacons, just prior to the exam results. Off we went in a convoy to Wales, where we drank hard and played hard. As the days progressed, I felt more and more tired, and it became extremely difficult for me climb stairs or walk very far without becoming breathless. My friends became concerned and took me to the accident and emergency department at Abergavenny Hospital. After numerous tests and ECG scans I was told that I was going to be kept in for observation because an X-ray image showed a dark mass over my heart.

That did not sound good, I thought.

I can't remember a great deal about my time in hospital, other than that I was very scared because no one could pin-point what was wrong with me. I recall that I had a lot of tests, and three days after I was admitted to hospital, I deteriorated and had to be rushed to the intensive care department. I remember being so hot that the nurses had to bring me a giant electric fan to cool me down. The last thing I remember was suddenly becoming freezing cold, then silence.

As I came back to consciousness, my mind told me that I was being strangled and so I began wrestling with, and swearing at, the four people who were bent over me. In reality, I was being given heart massage as my heart had stopped just seconds before. Coming into focus around my bed were the faces of concerned doctors and nurses, and my dad, who was holding my hand. It was the day of the A level results.

Sometime later, I remember asking about my A level results and dad telling me that I had done better than expected: I had achieved a grade B in French, two grades higher than my mock exams, six months previously. Thankfully I had secured my place at university, so I could stop worrying.

Over the course of the next 12 hours my heart stopped another two times. I had experienced death on three separate occasions and I was very ill indeed. Finally, with the hospital doctors completely at a loss as to what was wrong with me, I was rushed by ambulance up to the Queen Elizabeth Hospital in Selly Oak, Birmingham, where I was admitted to the coronary care unit and stayed for three months.

Eventually, after numerous tests, it was discovered that I had contracted a virus that attacked the inner muscle of my heart causing myocarditis. I was placed on an extremely powerful drug to prevent my heart from beating too fast, and I had an emergency operation to fit a pacemaker to prevent my heart from stopping altogether. I was also taking steroids to decrease the inflammation within the heart muscle. It was touch and go, and no one was sure that I would survive.

My daily life soon became a familiar routine of tests. I underwent three invasive tests within the heart itself. The doctors used a keyhole surgery technique to insert a wire into the main artery in my groin to feed leads into the heart to understand more about my condition. I was ordered to undergo complete bedrest for almost three months as I was not, under any circumstances, to exert my heart any more than was absolutely necessary to aid my recovery.

Life was never to be the same again. Over time, I defied the odds and got better, the virus receded and I was able to begin gentle exertion again. It began with a symbolic walk around my bed – when I did this, everyone cheered. Over the next few weeks I began my recuperation with gentle exercise tests and longer walks, up and down the hospital corridors.

By then it was October and I had been in hospital since August. The day of my release was very emotional. I couldn't wait to go home, yet I had made some fantastic friends with the other patients, doctors and nurses. They truly had been amazing and saved my life. Dad picked me up on the day of my release and the first thing I wanted to do was to go to the Malvern Hills and reconnect with nature. It had always been such a special place for me. I spent almost an hour just looking out over the countryside spread out below me like a beautiful patchwork quilt. University had begun, but because of the illness and the fact that I was very weak, it was decided that it would be better for me to defer my place for a year. So, I spent the next 12 months recuperating.

While the hospital staff were amazing and saved my life, they had merely fixed the physical issue. It was the huge swathe of mental scarring that I had as a result of my experience that was to create a lot of problems for me. I was released into a world where my mind became my over-protector. Because of what I'd been through, for many years I would be listening to every single beat of my heart, my ego-protector on red alert, just in case. It was absolutely exhausting and threw me into a pit of anxiety and despair; what doctors would today recognise as depression. Left without help, my mind raced off to do exactly what it wanted to do, without rational thought or logic. I became paranoid about my health, and my usual carefree attitude towards life disappeared.

On the anniversary of my 'death' (August 1991) I made my way downstairs at home very upset, hoping to reach out for some understanding. Unfortunately it was not forthcoming. I will not repeat what was said to me here within the pages of this book because I do not wish to give any more energy to it than is needed, but I have to tell this story as this incident alone shaped my future choices. At the time, I remember feeling crushed and totally alone. I had absolutely no one to talk to, nobody who understood. I vowed never to speak of my feelings or illness ever again to anyone – family or friends. I was the one who offered support and advice to everyone else, yet that support was never there for me. I retreated further into myself, keeping everything locked up inside for fear of being hurt again.

University was a just month away, and while I was scared to death, I couldn't wait to go. I took my deferred place and threw myself into my course. The course took me to France for 12 months, allowing me to meet some fantastic people who I had an absolute ball with. It also gave me the opportunity to spend 12 months in industry, working with more amazing people. I can honestly say that I had never had more fun.

When the time came to finish university I had nowhere to live, so I went back home, which was very difficult after spending four years free from parental control and restrictions.

It was now the mid-1990s and the UK was just coming out of recession. Graduate jobs were thin on the ground, so I applied for anything. After hundreds of applications I ended up working for a small components firm in the Black Country, hating every minute of it. Within 10 months I'd had enough and successfully applied for a marketing position with a local computer firm. Around this time I also became engaged to a lovely man I had met during my work placement year. We had plans to marry in September 1996 and we bought a house in readiness for our married life together. My parents were traditionalists, preferring that I waited to get married before I lived with my fiancé. We got married and settled down into a comfortable life, going to work, coming home, eating dinner in front of the TV, seeing friends and family at the weekends. We were comfortable together, but were never going to set the world alight.

In 1998 I secured a job at a local university as a Placements Officer. The pay was decent so my husband and I could relax more about paying our bills. At the end of 1998, the company where I had worked as a marketing assistant prior to the university job invited me to their Christmas party. Little did I know, that night my life was about to change forever.

This was the time that my spiritual journey began in earnest. Looking back, I believe that if I had been more aware, it could have started in August 1990 following my near death experiences; however, it was not meant to be. As I walked into the function room at the party and made my way to the bar, I was accosted by a man who I had known in passing and who looked very pleased to see me. We struck up a conversation and didn't stop talking all night. I felt I had known him forever, in this life, and all of my others. I have since found out what a twin flame is, and Jason is it.

I woke up the next morning feeling very strange. I knew that something awesome had happened to me, yet I couldn't put my finger on it. I began to feel extremely philosophical about life, searching for answers to deep questions about what makes us human and whether there is a divine plan for everyone living on the planet. Strange things were happening to my thought processes and so I took myself into the library signing out a huge pile of books on traditional philosophy. What I hadn't realised at the time was that I was looking for books on spiritual philosophy, authors like

Deepak Chopra, Wayne Dyer and countless others like them within the mind/body field. However, I truly believe that if I had discovered these books at that time, my development would have been too quick and I wouldn't have been able to cope.

I kept thinking about Jason. We had swapped phone numbers and email addresses, and we began emailing each other. We totally connected on everything, our sense of humour, our likes and dislikes, our vision for the future. It was amazing.

We could talk for hours and it felt like only a few minutes had passed. We greedily drank from each other's company.

Over time, it became clear that I was falling in love with Jason, and he with me. The situation was far from ideal. I was married. What was happening to me? Yet I couldn't stop seeing Jason. We knew we had a deep connection, a soul connection, it literally felt like he was me and I was him. I felt it, I knew it in every fibre of my being and he felt it too.

We knew what each other was going to say before we said it. We were deeply telepathically linked; I had never felt anything like this before. It was like something out of a fantasy novel or film.

I yearned to be with Jason all the time. Relations with my husband were not good; we barely spoke. We got on with each other in a comfortable way, but it wasn't anything like the million watts of electricity and chemistry that Jason and I created when we were together. I knew that our marriage wasn't working but how on earth could I leave? After almost four years of heart-rending passion and pain, my body helped the situation along. It couldn't cope any longer with the stress, worry or anxiety and gave way to a nervous breakdown. I remember making a call to my mother in total panic and distress about half way home from work one evening. I had parked in a lay-by, shaking physically, not even able to recall my own name. I remember that mom gently coaxed me via the loudspeaker of my mobile phone to drive back to my village, guiding me to remain calm and to drive directly to my doctor where she would make sure that dad was waiting for me.

The doctor took one look at me and confirmed that I had experienced a severe panic attack, brought on by prolonged stress and anxiety. He prescribed antidepressants and told me to return in seven days.

The next few weeks are a total blur to me. Somehow I continued to go to work, as I didn't think that my condition was as bad as it was, and I refused a sick note. My husband looked after me as best he could, but obviously no one was able to offer help or support as I couldn't tell them the truth about why I had experienced a nervous breakdown.

Finally I told my mom that things were not good between me and my husband, and that I wanted to move out. She asked if there was anyone who would be prepared to take me in, so I contacted a good friend of mine, who very kindly offered me a room. I stayed with her for a couple of months at the end of 2001/2002, deciding that I wanted a divorce and a new life.

The universe has always supported me throughout my life and given me exactly the right opportunities at the right time so it certainly didn't let me down now. I had just applied for a new job as a Careers Adviser in the careers service at the university and got the job after a very challenging interview. Celebrating this new position, I also realised that I needed to find a place to live as the marital home was to be sold as a result of the divorce. At this time, an advert appeared in the university news bulletin looking for live-in Student Hall of Residence Supervisors. I applied, went for the interview and got the position.

I moved into student halls in April 2002, started divorce proceedings and began a new job. Usually, just one of these traumatic events causes enough stress to manifest illness in the physical body, yet I had introduced all three of these life-changing events into my life at the same time.

My divorce was made final in September 2002, the house was sold, my new job began and I welcomed a new batch of undergraduates into my care in halls. Life was stressful and very different. In order to blot out the reality of the situation I would binge drink whenever I could, to numb the pain.

Jason and I had become very close. In fact, we had decided to go away for 10 days to Benidorm and when we returned, he became a permanent fixture in my little flat in student halls. It was worth all the pain and upset just to be with him, yet we now had another major problem looming on the horizon. Our parents were not happy that Jason and I were together, and we almost lost contact with them for two years as they were not able to support our relationship. This obviously caused a great deal of pain and heartache, and because of all the pressure, I developed a physical problem within my heart (atrial fibrillation). When I had an episode, I would be incapacitated, unable to speak or stand and it would also affect my vision. Because my heart was pumping irregularly, not enough blood was getting around my body. This condition was awful, as I never knew when an episode was going to take place. I would drive myself insane with worry and my ego-protector kicked back in again even more powerfully than before, giving me no break at all from the worry and anxiety about my health and whether my body was going to let me down again.

Eventually the stress of living in student halls and holding down a full-time job became too much, so Jason and I decided to move in together officially and rent a flat away from the university. We could not have been happier together, but everything else in our lives seemed to be going wrong. Perhaps it was karma as a result of our falling in love, who can tell? Our parents eventually came around to the idea of us being together, but not before Jason and I eloped to the Cotswolds to get married with just two witnesses as guests. It was the best day of my life.

At this point in my life, my health was steadily deteriorating. We had discovered holistic therapies as a way to complement my medical care and felt so connected to them that we decided to study them deeper. Over this period of several years we achieved Crystal Therapy, Reiki Master, Indian Head Massage, EFT (Emotional Freedom Techniques) and NLP (Neuro Linguistic Programming) qualifications.

As a result of the atrial fibrillation I was taking high doses of heart medication. On top of that, my emotional and mental state was extremely fragile and I spent my whole day worried about leaving the radius of the hospital, just in case I had an 'attack'. I became a virtual recluse in my own home and developed deep depression and anxiety. I lived in constant fear of my body letting me down, and wouldn't go anywhere on my own.

Many of my friends and family do not know this about me. On the outside I was 'happy go lucky' Louise, but on the inside I was in so much emotional pain and turmoil. The only person who knew exactly how I felt was Jason; he was my rock, and without him I don't know where I would be right now.

I had become very tired of life and often it was very hard to carry on, but somewhere deep inside I knew that I had been spared from dying at 18 years of age because I had to complete something. My ego finally let go, it was exhausted, and at that moment I reached out and knew that something had to change. I was living in permanent fear and anxiety, only gaining any respite when I was asleep.

When I began to really open my eyes, from the early 2000s onwards, life presented me with wonderful people, synchronicities and angelic helpers that have supported me to heal my life and body. With their help I have also achieved a deeper understanding about our place here on the Earth, as spiritual beings having a human experience. I realised that I was creating all the experiences within my life, just by the choices that I was making. This understanding freed me from my self-made prison and helped me to change my life for the better. If I look back now, I couldn't have sunk any lower and my only way was up.

I took a deep journey inside, and through my own intuition and inner guidance, mentors, books and therapies, I learnt over time that all the choices I ever made in my life were made out of fear as I didn't know of any other way. I was permanently worrying: what if this happens? what if that happens? This constant worry was creating stress in my whole body, resulting in physical and emotional dis-ease.

After being awakened to the spiritual path, I have been working hard on peeling the onion of my life, to try to understand why I manifested illness and the trials into my life that I did. I have undergone two further heart operations; laser ablations to remove scar tissue from the inside of my heart muscle that create arrhythmias. I have also committed to delving deep into my body and soul to uncover the nuggets of times past that were covered over and buried long ago, to retrieve the pieces of the puzzle and begin to uncover the precious treasure at the bottom of my experiences – my blueprint for my incarnation here on Earth.

From a place of severe anxiety and depression, I have managed to pick myself up and create a new life for myself. I now have excellent health, wonderful relationships with friends and family and do a job that I love every day, running my own therapy and training business. My life could not be more different, or better.

Along my journey, I learnt that all of the experiences that I have had in life were a result of choosing a fear response and disconnecting from the natural flow of my life; living in fear and resisting everything that came my way. I shut down my heart to feeling love or joy, and my quest over the past 10 years has been to rediscover these, slowly learning to view the world in a different way and to make choices from love rather than fear, reconnecting me to happiness and wellness.

It has been a truly cathartic experience putting each significant step of my journey down in written form in this book. Everything that happened and how I reacted to what happened shaped my health and wellness. I now choose to create my experiences from love and acceptance, realising that while I might not be able to control events around me, I can control how I react to them in a loving and peaceful way. I am now in a place where I am truly thankful and grateful for the amazing people and experiences that have come into my life, and have chosen to let any painful memories go with love and joy in my heart. For without them, I wouldn't be the person that I am today.

Jason's story

My mother gave birth to a large, chubby and healthy baby boy, weighing 10lb 8oz (4.7kg) to be precise.

My first breath announced that I had arrived. I started this incarnation as the product of a one-parent family, living on a sprawling and troubled post-war housing estate.

My mother had now increased the size of her brood to three; previously giving birth to my two older half sisters. I did not have much contact with my father as I grew up; I have faded memories of him appearing from time to time, as if by magic, in the living room on his way to work, only to leave soon after.

My first dalliance with academia was a very ordinary primary school at the bottom end of 'the estate'. Life had been settled and idyllic, spending time with my family 24/7 and playing in my own imaginary world. My mother had not sent me to a nursery, as was common in those days. Arriving at school I was welcomed into the reception class and proceeded to hide under the desk until I was collected. Why was I here? Why had I been abandoned for the day? Why was I taken to this noisy place away from my toys, my mother and my sanctuary? Mentally scarring me, I never really enjoyed school and would tell my mother that I didn't want to attend. Wanting to please me, she never forced or coerced me to go to school; she would sit me in front of the television to watch the school programmes, and these I would soak up like a sponge. I still remember them today, programmes such as *Picture Box* with Alan Rothwell, *You and Me* with the crow and hamster and *Look and Read* with the strange red and black foam 'Wordy'.

Mesmerised by these programmes and others, my mother made sure I was getting an education. When the school programmes finished for the day, I would play with Action Men, toy soldiers, cars and my favourite pastime – drawing. Although money was very tight in my family I was always furnished with paper, pencils and colouring books. I would spend hours lost in my own fantasies, creating landscapes and entire worlds. I would draw and draw and draw. It has never, even today, lost its appeal. To say that I was a sensitive child is an understatement. I did not want to mingle with others outside my world and was happy in the sanctuary afforded by my family.

My favourite time was sitting on the settee with a bottle of orange cordial, watching television and playing games with my imaginary friends. Life could get no better than this. I rejoiced at being in my own world. I knew eventually that I would have to go to school, but always tomorrow. In those days, truancy officers did not have anything to prove, no axe to grind or grudges to bear. I remember that the local officer would appear occasionally and question my mother. Giving the truthful and honest answer she would tell them that her son did not want to go to school. Unsure of exact events, as they did not directly involve me, she never went to prison, court, or had any action taken against her. This would be unheard of today, as the system wishes to punish and control free spirits and sensitive children by punishing parents who are often oblivious and ignorant of their children's actions. School days rolled around soon enough. When I did attend school I always found it oppressive, containing and bewildering.

1977 was the year of Queen Elizabeth II's silver jubilee. Street parties took place throughout the UK; our own street hosted a plethora of local children, some I recognised others I did not. There was a contest for the best costume, and as usual in working class areas with little or no money, all costumes were made by hand in a sort of make do approach. My mother dressed me as a little king. I recall looking quite dashing in a long red cape, with an orb and sceptre sprayed gold.

Adorned in handmade costumes, families swarmed to the street party, taking their places at the largest and longest table I had ever seen. Taking my place at the table, I proceeded to 'dig in' and ate my first sausage roll. The local servers rushed manically around the table piling more and more food onto each child's plate; little mouths could not hope to keep pace.

I recall my mother telling me throughout life to 'eat everything on your plate; starving children would give their right arm for that food'. This statement rang through my head;

eat, eat, eat. I had consumed copious amounts of party food for a small child, eating and stuffing every corner of my stomach to bursting point and still it came. Eventually the plate was emptied. My fancy dress costume won a prize, but instead of feeling joy and pride, a strange queasiness was building in my very full and amply stuffed stomach. Suddenly half-digested sandwiches, mingled with custard, biscuit and Angel Delight appeared from nowhere. I was violently sick, and as any five-year-old would, I cried and cried.

My first experience of bullying was at the hands of a local boy who lived on my street; I could see where he lived from my mother's front room. As children do, we would ride bikes and play games, yet one eventful day we argued, over what, I can't remember, but he was unusually mean to me. This single event was to change my life for ever; running inside I told my mum. Instead of making me stand up for myself she took charge, intervened, resolved the situation and I resumed my idyllic life. Little did I know that if I had dealt with this incident myself, my life would have been very different and I would not be the person telling you this story today.

At an early age, my life was shaped by the various children who occupied 'the grove'. I would join in with various games, mingling with both quiet and rowdy children. Weekends and long summer holidays meant being picked last for teams and stuck in goal during football. Being rather a portly child I can clearly see that my interests in sports were extinguished at this very point in my development. One day I recall thinking 'I'm always in goal, I never get picked, I never play'; but never gave any more thought to the matter. The year came and went and I remember riding my bike; a red and black Raleigh. Some of the children found it highly amusing to place twigs and sticks in my wheels catapulting me over the handle bars. Nursing an injury I decided that I would retreat to the sanctuary of my home and cocoon myself in my own safe world.

The long hot summer of 1978 saw me making what I thought was a good friend. As we played one day, we met with an older boy who I did not know. I had been given a glorious orange and black ball; the older boy threw my ball into a large lump of dog mess and both he and my 'friend' simply ran off laughing. Standing there, I was alone and had little choice but to retrieve my ball. How cruel and unjust I found the world; arriving home in floods of tears I told my mother what had happened and once again she sorted it out.

School and home life continued in much the same vein for several years. I was now 11 years old and preparing for senior school at the local comprehensive school. I settled into my allotted form and met my classmates and made some friends. I took classes such as history and French; the former I excelled in, the latter I had no talent for. Suddenly, my life was to change and not for the better. A sustained barrage of abuse and bullying, physical and mental by a hulking figure with a huge chip on his shoulder, singled me out. This bullying was to last for several years. Days at school were spent looking over my shoulder and living in fear of whether or not I was to arrive home covered in bruises.

Looking back I see the patterns: problems with my playmates and problems at school. This had plagued my life and was commonplace. My solution, as usual, was to run and hide, sometimes being found and when I was, always being hit. Choosing not to fight back, gripped by fear and anguish and sinking into despair and depression, I tried to hold it together for two years and until one day I could bottle it up no longer. In desperation, I once again turned to my mother; she had sorted everything else out in my life, how could she not sort this out? Meeting after meeting took place with the school, but to no avail. The bullying continued and to some extent got worse. Bullying was seen as 'character building' and was something that 'you just went through'. I suppose this is true, it does build character and it has made me into who I am today, moulding my sense of right and wrong.

One evening my knee buckled under my body weight and the pain was excruciating. Several X-rays later Osgood-Schlatter syndrome was diagnosed. My leg was confined to a cast and I was effectively housebound. All I could feel was joy to be out of an environment where I was constantly looking over my shoulder and not having to deal with the bullying. Home tutoring saw me advance academically, I forged ahead of the rest of my classmates with just three hours of teaching per week. My knee eventually recovered and after physiotherapy I returned to school, to the bullying and 'normal' life.

Concerned with my lack of self-confidence and ability to defend myself I started martial arts classes and showed a flair for them; I felt great. Eventually I finished school and moved onto college to study engineering. Even though I could now defend myself, I still looked over my shoulder as I did not want any confrontation. The emotional scarring of those experiences still haunted my daily life. However, thankfully, never in four years did I have to deal with a bully.

Following college I applied to study an engineering degree. Over the next four years, I completed my degree and continued on to a master's degree in software systems engineering. Bullying appeared to be a thing of the past, or so I thought.

After university I took several jobs; none really fulfilling. Then I happened to see an advert for a programming tutor in a local paper. I applied and secured the position, responsible for mail and telephone guidance, running workshops and preparing materials for new courses. The manager exhibited her background in the armed forces adequately while running the department. This position was always intended as a short-term stopgap while I looked for another software engineering job. However, I found that I liked teaching and I stayed in the academic arena; which was where I felt most comfortable.

Bullying soon raised its head again; both from management and colleagues. Two fellow tutors, with whom I initially formed a close bond, were the main perpetrators. They would socialise, speak in coded language, share 'in' jokes; cunningly involving me in conversations then tittering and scoffing between themselves at my responses. Soon relationships inevitably broke down between us. I had no one to fight my corner and I could not expect to sort this out the usual way; I was a grown man. But my natural condition was to want to retreat, to have things sorted out.

Instead of facing the issues I decided to move position and look for another job, subconsciously side stepping them. The universe was presenting me with yet another chance to end cycles, but at this point I just could not see this. My employment as a tutor lasted for just over three years and was to pave the way for a high calibre professional teaching position, where I would find happiness, a new utopia, or so I thought.

I had been undertaking a Certificate in Education at a local college and one evening the tutor announced that the college needed staff for evening classes in computing. This would be great to supplement my income and I decided to apply. I was interviewed for the position and was offered a job as a full-time lecturer in computing. With renewed vigour and drive, I tended my resignation to my current employer to begin my lecturing post. Settling into my job I found a natural rapport with the students. I had also started to see Louise, now my wife, who was then married to her first husband.

We had both worked for my previous employer and met at the photocopier; an immediate spark between us was evident. The first time we talked properly was at a work colleague's wedding and I remember thinking that she was someone very special. Later we met at a Christmas office party and talked insanely all evening. Shortly after this we both left our jobs, she for a post at a local University and me for the college. I remember that I would travel to the university to spend time with her, as friends at first, due to the situation with her marriage, then later as a couple.

I recall the day that Louise announced she was leaving her husband. We both agreed that we would like to live together but the situation was not ideal. Those days were not good for Louise or me and we both slipped in and out of deep depression; the only people we could talk to and rely upon were each other. We would try to cheer each other up, lifting each other's moods, sometimes to no avail. Life rolled on like this for several months, secretly seeing each other as a couple, meeting for drinks and companionship. All the time, we were ripped apart when we had to go our separate ways at the end of the evening.

Louise and I had been seeing each other for a while now, she had moved out of her marital home and was living in University halls of residence as a hall tutor; a pastoral care role. My lecturing job was going well but, after the events of recent years, a holiday was long overdue. Boarding the plane for 10 days in the sun and getting away from England meant that we could be a proper couple, no skulking and no hiding. We did the classic English tourist things, walking, sunning and drinking so much that we forgot days from our life. Arriving back in England we realised that we could not bear to be parted; we'd had such a good time and each found our 'soul mate'. I moved into Louise's small and cosy flat, returning home only to gather clothes and occasionally eat. It was at this point that the relationship between me and my mother started to deteriorate to the point of destruction.

How different this situation was. The preceding New Year I had taken Louise home to meet my mother. We were going out to celebrate at a local nightclub and my mother had really taken a shine to Louise. As is customary, and being young, Louise and I drank too much and ended up virtually walking home. Louise took my bed while I slept on the sofa. But now my mother could not resolve the fact that I was moving out of the family home. I was not seen as an individual who could have his own life, have his own needs and wants.

Unfortunately, my mother began to control me, doing and saying just what she liked to me, just like everyone else in my life. Who did the small child inside me turn to for support now? The one person who was my saviour had now switched her role, becoming extremely nasty and vindictive towards me. I felt as though I did not want to be around her. The relationship with my mother completely disintegrated and I did the only thing that I could do, I retreated. Failing to stand up for myself, choosing to take the easy route, evade and escape, I withdrew to the only person who truly understood me

– Louise. Other than Louise, I felt totally alone in the world. It was a tough time and I sank further into depression.

At work, our department was relocated to another part of the college and a new line manager was appointed. This promotion of our colleague brought power and intimidation; bullying of staff under his control became commonplace. It was always carried out on the quiet, talking to us in locations where no witnesses were present. For nearly four years this manager would employ psychological tactics, a word here a word there, undermining people and especially me. He was perfectly positioned to change my life forever. I began to dread going into work, feeling sick and anxious in the pit of my stomach.

The following years saw me marry Louise and become her carer. She was suffering palpitations and a heart condition, due partly to the stress of her divorce and an old heart condition that she had when she was younger. Stress is a funny thing and can manifest at any time, just like delayed shock. Our lives were a long series of hospital visits, 24 hour observational tapes, medication reviews and heart ablations that have seen her recover and lead a normal life.

It was a very difficult time, watching the woman I love go through such challenging circumstances, powerless to do anything about it. I was supposed to protect her and keep her safe from harm but this was simply not going to happen, my world was spinning out of control. I recall waking at all hours to help Louise with anxiety attacks, trying to ease them before they spiralled into palpitations. I would listen for the tone in her voice that meant that everything was not as it should be. This was the way that life was taking us, and over time it had become perfectly normal. While I coped on the outside, giving Louise the confidence and support she needed, inside I was falling apart.

At college things were getting worse and worse.

December 2008, found me in a corridor alone with my manager only to experience yet more inappropriate remarks. Finally something snapped, I had been undermined for four years and suffered incessant mental abuse. I remember going home, going to bed and sleeping for the whole weekend. The thought of going back to work on Monday made me feel physically sick. From that day onwards I never returned and was signed off work suffering from depression and anxiety as a result of work-related stress.

After much soul searching, I took the difficult decision to make a formal grievance against my manager; finally taking responsibility and control for what was happening to me. The college initiated an investigation, concluding that there was no real evidence to go any further. An appeal was launched and an in-depth investigation was commenced by senior staff. Unfortunately the result of this investigation was, once again, no wrong doing and finding little or no evidence for bullying.

I'd had enough, I wrote my notice and resigned my post. Finally, I understood what the universe was trying to tell me. I had found the strength (even though depressed and deflated) to stand up for myself, to correct all of the bullying incidents in my past. With the tendering of my resignation, I turned my attention to my mother and family. Mustering the same resolve, I stood up to them and outlined how they had impacted me throughout my life. It is heartening for me that as a result of this, my relationship with my mother is much better.

After finding myself in a place of deep depression and anxiety, like Louise, the only way for me was back up. Through my therapies and discovering ancient spiritual philosophy, over time I succeeded in changing my view of the world, realising that the only person who could change my life was me. I began to look at the world differently and realise that we all have a choice regarding how we react when life throws us a curved ball. I am now living a happy and healthy life, running a training and therapy business with Louise and enjoying every minute. Life is good.

Without the events described as part of my story, this book would never have been born. I have learnt that throughout the whole of my life I never stood up for myself to stop the bullying and I made choices from fear. The moment that I wrote my notice and submitted it, I immediately corrected all the events of the past. I stood up for the little Jason's, all of them throughout my life, who never raised their voices and took the easy route. I ended those cycles. Therefore, I would like to say a big 'thank you' to every single one of those bullies who brought me all of those experiences; without them I would not have been able to reach this amazing time in my life and end those cycles.

We hope that our stories, and the suggestions for your personal development journey contained within this book, will inspire and motivate you to move towards creating health, happiness and wellness within your own lives. We bring these philosophies and understandings to you in a non-religious context, helping you to reconnect and access your existing inner understanding.

We present to you now, the understanding that has supported us to move from a place of fear into one of love and acceptance. We have worked hard on changing our view of the world around us, moving from a viewpoint of fear and stress, to seeing the world and our experiences within it as beautiful; abundant in health, happiness and wellness. We finally dissolved the self-sabotage and limiting beliefs in our minds, to enable us to focus our attention exactly how and where we choose – doing this step stone by step stone.

I AM important
and my story
deserves to
be told.

YOUR STORY

'If you bring forth that which is within you, then that which is within you will be your salvation.

If you do not bring forth that which is within you, then that which is within you will destroy you.'

The Gnostic Gospels

You are a product of all of your experiences to date. Those experiences shimmer like jewels along the pathway of your life. While you may label those experiences at the moment as 'good' or 'bad', as a result of the choices that you made, each of them has taught you something along the way and you wouldn't be who you are right now without them. These experiences, and how you reacted to them, had an immediate effect on your health and wellness.

As you progress through life, you paper over earlier experiences and begin to build them up, layer upon layer, reacting in specific ways to what happens to you. Remember Jason attracting bullying incidents into his life and feeling anxiety and fear until one day he learnt to choose differently, from a place of love. Also remember Louise, attracting illness into her life until she learnt to choose her reaction differently, viewing her experiences as gifts, learning from them from a place of acceptance. By reacting differently, the pattern of negativity can be broken.

Those experiences were always going to happen, it was how we dealt with them that was the key to our wellness, or not, at the time.

Exactly who and where you are right now on your journey is OK; there is no judgement or retribution here. Take the pressure off yourself by disgarding labels and judgement; allow yourself to 'be' and simply tell your story, getting to know yourself again in the process. Identify what specific events shaped you and the decisions that you make today as a result.

The pathway back to health and wellness and the magnificent you that you are, is to gently peel away those layers like an onion, until you uncover your true self by telling your story. This is done at a pace that is comfortable and safe for you, without judgement. Your story is the key to your health and wellness.

ACTIVITY

If you feel you are ready and able, begin to note down all of those experiences in life which you believe have shaped you and made you who you are today, as a result of choices that you made. Whether at this stage you perceive them to be good or bad is not of concern, so please do not judge yourself harshly. Later on in the book you will begin to reflect on these experiences and use them to help you to understand the kinds of choices you make and why you perceive life in the way that you do.

We found that when you open yourself up to any new concepts, particularly when they focus your attention on sometimes difficult memories or areas of your life, it is important that you are appropriately resourced and supported in order to help you to get the most out of this work. What follows are some suggestions that we found supported us in integrating new philosophies and ways of being into our world:

- Surround yourself with like-minded people who share your interests, who feel comfortable to be around and who you can really talk to about anything without being judged.
- Spend five minutes each day focusing on your breathing, allow thoughts to come and go (do not concern yourself with them), simply allowing yourself to 'be'.

- Do things that make you happy – watching a comedy, reading an uplifting book, going for a walk in nature.
- Get plenty of rest.
- Think about supporting your development with the help of a good holistic therapist.
- Delete negative labels and judgement of yourself and others – allow yourself to 'be'.

These are simple suggestions, designed to support you to gently regain your inner strength and begin to learn to reconnect to the flow of life as you work through this book at a pace that is right for you.

ACTIVITY

FOLLOWING THE BREATH

Without breathing we would die within a few minutes, it is the life force that sustains us. It is our connection to the universe and everything within it. This activity demonstrates that we are always connected. We are always supported, whatever might be happening within our world at the time.

Find a quiet place where you will not be disturbed. Make yourself comfortable, play some soothing music and close your eyes. Start to become conscious of your breath. Breathe in slowly and breathe out, rhythmically. Continue to do this for about five minutes, feeling the breath enter and exit, bringing life force to your body. When you are ready, come back to the room, stretch and open your eyes.

It is suggested that you spend five minutes each day in quiet contemplation of the breath. Over time, you allow subtle changes to occur on deeper energetic levels, helping you to feel more calm and at peace with life.

We wish to end this chapter by saying that while your story has shaped you and the person that you are, *your biography does not have to mean your destiny.*

You have the power to change anything and everything in your life and connect to your full potential, inner serenity and wellness, if that is what you so desire.

I choose the path of love and peace.

Love – 'An intense feeling of deep affection. A great interest or pleasure in something.'

Fear – 'An unpleasant emotion caused by the threat of danger, pain, or harm.'

Oxford English Dictionary

Whether you are aware of them or not, the emotions of love and fear are all around us every second of the day. Think about a typical day in your life for a moment.

1. The alarm clock rings to tell you that it's time to get up – are you excited about your day ahead and skip out of bed to the shower, or are you filled with dread? Do you throw the covers over your head and go back to sleep?

2. You are sitting at the breakfast table and your partner, child or pet comes to see you – how do you feel? Are you filled with love, or are you irritated at being disturbed?

3. You are sitting in a queue of traffic trying to get to where you need to be – do you sit back, relax and listen to your favourite radio station, or are you inwardly cursing the situation, worrying that you are going to be late?

4. You are reading your daily newspaper at lunchtime and every page is full of doom and gloom – do you toss the paper to one side and enjoy your lunch, or do you allow yourself to feel anxious because of the current state of the world?

5. You are watching the TV before bedtime and every advert is telling you that you must purchase the product being demonstrated because without it, you are not good enough or you won't be as good as your friends – do you turn down the sound, switch over and smile, or feel anxious because you don't have the product and vow to buy it at the earliest opportunity?

In the simple exercise above, it is clear that every choice we make produces either a sensation of love or fear within our body. While we cannot do anything about the outside influences, what is clear is that we do have a choice about what emotion to feel. What is not so easy, is knowing how to undo a lifetime of programming in which most of us have learnt to choose the emotion of fear, thereby creating anxiety and distress within our physical and emotional body. Let this acronym start to put fear into perspective:

FEAR – False Evidence Appearing Real

Our modern day world has contributed greatly to our choice of the fear response. The ways employed to do this are very powerful and play on our basic needs for protection, safety and survival, and have been expertly honed over many years. Just think for a moment about advertising. We are told that if we don't buy product X then we are bad people and putting ourselves or our families at risk, however, product X has the answer and can help you with your previously unknown 'problem'. We unconsciously allow the product to speak to our primal fears and subsequently react from fear, rather than from love, and as a result we create habit-based fear responses. Our daily serving of news is also geared to report the most sensational stories that it can. While there is no denying that terrible things can and do happen, these events need to be put into context along with the millions of acts of kindness and goodness that take place each and every second of every day. Remember, the media has immense power to shift the world's attention into one probable reality, but this does not have to be our own reality.

What is needed is perspective and awareness. From the point of perspective and being aware, you find the ability to listen to your body, your gut instinct and what you know to be true in your heart, not what everyone and everything around you is saying.

This, in context, is the key to your journey to wellness, to happiness, health and prosperity in all areas of your life.

From the beginning of this book, we want you to understand that you can become master of your own destiny again, free of boundaries and restrictions, and learn to trust what you know to be inherently true. We speak from experience and will provide you with simple techniques, which we have used successfully, to introduce you to deeper spiritual understanding and to support you with this transition.

Love and fear are very strong emotions. We knew what these words meant to us and the emotions that they created within us, but we wanted to find out what others understood by these terms. We asked a group of friends and students from our training school what words they would attribute to love and fear. The table shows what they said.

Love		Fear	
Joy	Happy	Angry	Hateful
Warm	Beautiful	Sad	Anxious
Kindness	Peace	Depressed	Stress
Gratitude	Bliss	Terrified	Distraught
Calm	Serene	Trembling	Jagged
Perfection	Smiling	Jittery	Upset
Appreciation	Gorgeous	Apprehensive	Cross
Delightful	Lovely	Hopeless	Distressed

We then asked the group to concentrate for a few short moments on the words they had picked when describing their understanding of fear, asking them to identify what they were feeling within their body. Here are the results:

- Stressed out and anxious with a tight feeling in the chest.
- An unpleasant, nauseous feeling in the stomach.
- Unpleasant memories surfacing from childhood.
- Feeling emotional.
- Fidgeting.
- Loss of control.

We then asked the group to concentrate for five minutes on the words chosen to convey what they understood by the word love. We asked them to feel the words in their body and to report back once complete. The results were as follows:

- Memories of long, happy summer days spent as a teenager with friends.
- A warm feeling in the heart.
- Can't stop smiling.
- Feeling calm and peaceful throughout the body.
- Quiet and happy.

When we asked the group what feelings they preferred from the exercise, all of them, without question, said that they preferred to concentrate on the words from the love column, as they felt so much better physically and emotionally when they did this.

As our very simple exercise shows, love and fear are extremely strong emotions. Our group commented that they were unaware just how powerful feeling love and fear was, when focusing on them in an isolated environment. Every day we experience love- or fear-based emotions, yet we probably don't recognise how powerful they are because we are so immersed in our everyday lives and these responses come out of our subconscious awareness. However, if we reflect on these emotions in isolation, and really give ourselves the time and the space to feel and acknowledge how they affect us physically and emotionally, we can understand how much of an impact these emotions are having on us on a daily basis and how, in turn, they can affect our health.

Love and fear are the only emotions that human beings are able to experience and communicate. Through our education and conditioning, we label other emotions such as joy, happiness and serenity or anger and hate, yet as we have seen above these are merely subcategories of the main emotions of love and fear.

The emotions of love and fear are at opposite ends of the scale, yet are equally as strong. Love can paralyse us, as can fear, yet if we attribute positive or negative feelings to these emotions, we would probably determine that love was a positive emotion, and fear negative.

There has been much research into the connection between mind and body by well known scientists, including Drs Bruce Lipton, Caroline Myss and Deepak Chopra, whose groundbreaking books prove with cutting-edge science how holistic approaches to health work, choosing to see the body from a quantum physics point of view, revealing that underneath our seemingly solid bodies, we are all composed of energy. When we say holistic, we mean looking at the body as a whole, incorporating the mind, body and spirit, rather than viewing all humans as a machine containing merely atoms and molecules. If modern day culture continues to look at the body as a mere machine, the most important part of the overall picture will continue to be missed.

So now let's take a fresh view of the world; allowing ourselves to bring the traditional Western view of health incorporating just the physical, together with the holistic view of the very real flow of energy that exists within each and every person. As we do this, we allow ourselves to understand that everything is connected. Scientific evidence now supports how our thoughts and beliefs give off vibrations that affect the entire energy field, creating the world that we sense around us.

By allowing ourselves to view health in this way, we can start to understand that if we create a fearful, negative electrical signal, then this will affect the chemistry within our body making us feel a particular way. If we refer back to the simple exercise we carried out with our friends and students at the beginning of this chapter, we can clearly see that all the words associated with fear invoked powerful and uncomfortable feelings within our group.

According to Dr Lipton, there are three causes for disruption in the healthy signalling of the body:

* Trauma: accidents cause a disruption in the brain signal.
* Toxins interfere with the body's signalling chemistry.
* The mind: if the mind sends inappropriate signals at the wrong times, our systems become imbalanced and diseased.

What Dr Lipton's work demonstrates is that any fear-related response disrupts the normal balance of the body and mind. If the response is maintained for a long time, the body's equilibrium is compromised. We can feel overloaded, emotionally blocked and eventually become sick. Prolonged feelings of negativity, which alter the natural equilibrium of the body, can accumulate over days, weeks and even years. While our minds may adjust to the incessant stresses occurring within our body, our bodies and their organs do not, and if this imbalance is left unchecked for too long sickness can manifest.

REFLECT

Considering the evidence, which of these emotions are you mostly living in on a day-to-day basis – love or fear? Are you able to pinpoint anything within your own story that has had a direct effect on the choices that you make?

It is true that love and hate cannot coexist, where there is one, there cannot be the other. Again, science has proved that if you allow yourself to think of a positive, loving emotion, then a gentle flowing vibration will be restored to the body's energy field. Doc Childre and Howard Martin, authors of *The HeartMath Solution*, conducted a spectral analysis study of heart rhythm data. They studied someone who was frustrated and looked at the frequency view of the person's heart rhythm while feeling that frustration. The results showed that when a person is frustrated, the frequency structure of the heart's rhythmic pattern becomes disordered or incoherent. This indicates disorder in the functioning of the autonomic nervous system. When the heart is operating in this disordered mode, it broadcasts an incoherent electromagnetic signal throughout the body and into the space around the person, which can be clearly measured.

In the same study, scientists monitored the heart rhythms of someone feeling sincere appreciation. The frequency pattern was shown to be very different from the person in the state of frustration. The study showed that when a person feels appreciation, the two branches of the autonomic nervous system work together with increased harmony to produce a single, coherent heart rhythm, meaning that an inner state of entrainment is at work. In this state of internal balance, the patterns in the electromagnetic field produced by the heart also become more coherent and harmonious.

The electromagnetic signature of the body is completely interdependent. If the mind perceives the fear response, the body reacts accordingly, with stress hormones flying about the bloodstream and the heart rhythm also affected. If left for a long time without rectifying and restoring balance and harmony, these imbalances begin to manifest physical conditions including migraine, digestive disorders and heart problems.

Dr David Hamilton, in his book *Why Kindness is Good For You*, highlights new scientific studies that show how acts of kindness, compassion and gratitude, produce chemicals in the brain that impact the body. One of these chemicals is a neuropeptide known as oxytocin, which travels out of the brain and into the bloodstream. Recent research shows that oxytocin is cardioprotective, which means that it protects the heart from damage, as it is one of the chemicals responsible for dilating the arteries, allowing easier blood flow around the body. What this means is that when you choose the love response, you are actually doing your heart a lot of good.

Much of this new research has shown that a kind, loving nature reduces the chances of your arteries becoming hard. In 2008, a scientific study investigated the process of atherosclerosis and actually found that oxytocin, the chemical produced when you're kind to someone, halted it in its tracks.

ACTIVITY

If you are feeling anxious or fearful about an issue, try bringing an image or feeling to mind of happiness or contentment. Stay with this for at least five minutes and what you should begin to notice is that you cannot feel two emotions at the same time. If you feel under threat (a fear response) think about something that brings you joy and happiness and the fear will soon disappear.

It is worth noting that it does take time and effort to change your responses, particularly if you are prone to worry or fear responses. This book is designed to support you with this journey, so be patient and kind to yourself as you travel your own path of development.

At this juncture, we also want to share with you the effect that the fear- or love-based response has on water. There has been extensive research carried out on the subject of water, and its ability to hold memory. A scientist called Masaru Emoto has researched and written several books concerning messages that can be held within water. Dr Emoto carried out water crystal experiments, exposing water contained in glasses to different words, pictures or music. He then froze the water and examined the aesthetics of the resulting crystals with microscopic photography. What Dr Emoto found was that the water exposed to beautiful, loving words, sounds or pictures formed a geometric design that was beautifully shaped when frozen; rather like snowflakes when observed under a powerful microscope. On the other hand, water exposed to negative words, sounds or pictures demonstrated definite distortion and were randomly formed, many shard-like and ugly with no real symmetry. There is no denying how most of us feel when on the receiving end of a loving comment or embrace, and conversely how we feel when someone inflicts physical harm or uses violent language towards us. We certainly feel something in our body; one of those feelings is generally pleasant, the other is not.

There is some conjecture about how much water the human body contains – anything from 50% to upwards of 70% of our total body mass. However, there is no doubt that we comprise at least half water, and, if water does react in the way that Dr Emoto's experiments seem to suggest, then we can be sure that the water contained in our body will carry the imprint of either loving or fearful responses into our cells and affect us at the cellular level.

What is clear, from all the research presented in this chapter, is that fear- or love-based responses have a definite effect on the physical and energetic structure of the body, translating into feelings of dis-ease or wellness depending on the choice of response taken.

You will learn effective tools and techniques as you progress further through this book to help you to become more aware of the wonder that is you, and make a conscious choice as to which emotion you wish to feel. Learning to choose the path of love rather than fear, in any given situation, is the direct route to inner peace and happiness.

It is important to realise that we have a choice about how and what to feel every second of our lives. We cannot control external influences, but we do have total control over how we react and what feelings we choose to experience. Be kind to yourself while you are learning to integrate these new concepts into your world, and do not give up. Learning a new way of viewing the world, and a new way of being takes time, but enjoy the journey as you do so and don't give yourself a hard time if you react in an 'old' way. This will pass in time.

ACTIVITY

REVIEW YOUR DAY

What happened today? Did you make choices out of fear or out of love? Make some notes.

ANCHORING LOVE THROUGH YOUR HEART

This activity will support you to connect to inherent feelings of love, gratitude and bliss; helping you to strengthen your mind, body and soul.

Find a quiet space where you will not be disturbed for about 10 minutes. Make yourself comfortable and close your eyes. When you are ready, feel or see your heart filling up with golden light. The golden light is pure love, bliss and gratitude. Feel this love, bliss and gratitude filling up every available space in your heart. You may feel your heart grow warmer as you continue with this exercise. Stay in this beautiful heart space for as long as you feel comfortable knowing that you are perfectly safe and protected. You may begin to feel more at peace and relaxed. Radiate this wonderful feeling now through the whole of your body – see it or just feel it happening. As you do this, know that every cell of your being is filling with love, bliss and gratitude; relaxing into pure health and wellness. Stay with the feeling for a few more moments, then take three cleansing breaths, stretch and open your eyes.

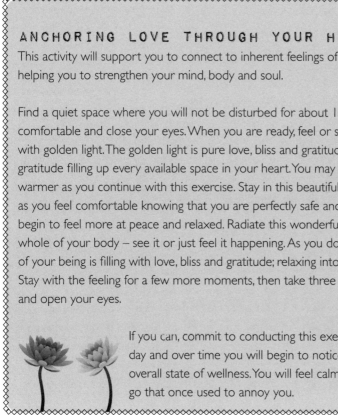

If you can, commit to conducting this exercise at least once per day and over time you will begin to notice the benefits to your overall state of wellness. You will feel calmer, more able to let things go that once used to annoy you.

Before we close this chapter, we wish to talk about beliefs, in particular those that limit. The reason for this is that while we now know that we have a choice about how we react – from a state of love or fear – those beliefs that we have about ourselves, created as a result of our upbringing and experiences throughout life, can block our access to those choices.

Limiting beliefs are thoughts or ideas that hold us back, firmly rooted in our behaviours built up from an event in the past, inherited from family, or based on the perceptions of others. Beliefs such as 'I am inadequate', 'Why would anyone want to love me?', 'I will never be successful, so why bother?', 'I am worthless', 'I am a loser', 'I am fat', and so many more.

As babies we are 'brand new'. We are a clean canvas that over time becomes painted with experiences. But right at the point of our birth we are totally connected to our infinite potential. Anything is possible because we have no experiences, no reference points to hold us back or protect us.

Wouldn't it be wonderful if we could reconnect to that?

ACTIVITY

WHEN DID EVERYTHING CHANGE?

As a result of writing down your story, now identify what you used to do in your life that you don't do now.

To give you an example, consider the story of a woman who is happily married and since bringing her children into the world has never done anything on her own or for herself. Almost two decades later the children are building lives of their own, and for the first time in years she begins to find that she has time for herself. Yet the anxiety that is caused by this new situation is overbearing. Does she have the confidence to go out on her own? She feels silly, and thinks back to her younger days when she would go clubbing until all hours and walk home on her own. She used to have no fear. Where did that woman go?

Work through your story, from birth right through to the present day. At what points in your life were you totally fearless? What did you do that you don't do now? What changed?

Limiting beliefs have been recently described as memes. Memes are ideas or a pattern of thought that replicate like a virus, infiltrating and spreading, unless stopped in their tracks. In this context, our limiting beliefs are viruses of the mind. Just think about those limiting beliefs that were created a long time ago in your life, that were allowed to replicate, infiltrate and spread, thereby dictating to you how you now live your life. This is not the way that life was meant to be and the sooner that these limiting beliefs, or viruses, can be eradicated, the better for your health and wellness.

Remember: the truth is that your limiting beliefs are not true.

By identifying your limiting beliefs and the labels you have about yourself, you begin to bring them into your conscious awareness, where they can be worked on and eliminated, thereby reconnecting you to your infinite potential. Every step stone presented here is designed to support you in viewing the world around you in a different way, if you choose to, and as a result of this beginning to change your limiting beliefs.

ACTIVITY

LIMITING BELIEFS

As a result of writing down your story, you are probably in a position to identify your limiting beliefs. Write every single one of these beliefs down on a sheet of paper. Be kind to yourself and take as much time as you need, ensuring you do not judge yourself or reproach yourself in any way.

By the side of each of these beliefs write the sentence 'This belief is NOT TRUE!' You must understand that the limiting beliefs you have about yourself are completely untrue.

Once you have completed the exercise, consciously allow yourself to disassociate from all the limiting beliefs and labels that you have written. You don't have to keep these inside any more because in this exercise you have removed them from your physical self and placed them on a sheet of paper.

When you are ready, fold up the paper and find a safe place to put it, in a box or envelope. We will come back to this exercise later on, but for now, give yourself some space, some room to breathe, and experience life without those beliefs and labels. Allow yourself to find out who you truly are and reconnect with the infinite potential that has always been there within you.

You can create a new view of your world that is abundant with empowering beliefs; over time replacing your old, outdated beliefs with new ones that support and nurture you.

Regardless of who you are right now as a result of experiences, limiting beliefs or the labels that you or others have given yourself, it is possible to reconnect with your health and wellness and achieve your maximum potential.

If you used to be fearless and drive all over the country on your own or do any number of wonderful things, yet you believe you can't now; let us tell you that you can.

From previous chapters we know that you are always connected to everything you ever need – your potential.

You are already free to be magnificent.

Your biography is not your destiny, so throw away those limiting beliefs and labels. Be ready to embrace what you have always been, a brilliant being of serenity, peace and wellness.

YOUR JOURNEY SO FAR:

- Your biography is not your destiny.
- You are free to make choices.
- Your health and wellness are affected by the choices you make; therefore it is important to be consciously aware of the choices you make, and to put these choices into perspective.
- The limiting beliefs you have about yourself are not true.

I choose to turn my attention to those things that serve me best.

'If you change the way you look at things; the things you look at change'

Wayne Dyer

It is true that if we change the way we look at things, the things we look at change, *however, we can only change that which we are truly aware of.*

The study of NLP has shown that, in general, the conscious mind can only handle seven (plus or minus two, i.e. five, seven or nine) bits of information at any given time. This means that millions of other bits of information, external influences and our own thoughts and feelings are going straight into our subconscious if they do not make it into our conscious awareness. Obviously there is a reason for this. If we didn't actively select information all the time, we would end up with too much information coming in and become overloaded. This is why we filter information through a variety of ways including our beliefs, values and memories.

Over time, we relegate most of our regular decisions to the default, subconscious mind, and this is why many of us become caught in a loop that we can never seem to free ourselves from, acting in the same way out of habit. Until, that is, we become consciously aware again of those things in our lives that we want to change.

By becoming more consciously aware of the choices that we make on a daily basis, we are in a perfect position to make a conscious choice as to how we react to the circumstances that appear within our lives.

At this point you should have a greater conscious awareness about what kind of choices you make on a daily basis, following on from the 'Review your day' activity in the previous chapter.

- Are your choices fear-based or made from a positive, loving standpoint?
- Were you aware of the type of choices that you were making?
- Has this understanding shocked you? Why?
- Did you make these choices instinctively? Did you consciously think about them beforehand, or do you always fall into the same pattern of response?
- Of the fear-based choices, what were they specifically related to (work, family, survival)?

REFLECT

Have you identified any patterns?
Is there a particular area of your life that is causing you to react in a more fear-based way?
What parts of your life are you reacting to in a loving way?
What part of your life story do you believe affects the decisions that you make today?

By completing this activity you begin to become consciously aware of the choices that you make and to bring into your awareness exactly which camp they fall into – fear-based or love-based. As we discovered in the previous chapter, choices made out of fear affect the chemistry of the body and result in feelings of anxiety or stress. In contrast, it is interesting to note that choices made out of love also affect the chemistry of the body, but in a positive way, producing hormones, including oxytocin, which have been proven to protect the heart and allow more blood flow through the arteries.

In our own personal experiences and as a result of working closely with our clients, what has become clear is that many people choose the same responses because of the body's default programming. Over a long period of time they have always reacted in a particular manner and eventually they don't know of any other way to react, so they continue to act in the same way until that method no longer works for them.

We continued to make choices from our default, fear-based position until our health suffered and we were forced to look for a healthier way of living or risk serious illness.

Working together and supporting each other, we discovered that we were making fear-based choices with little or no rationale as to why this was the case. We realised, and became aware, that the choices we made were conducted with no conscious thought, as though guided by an unseen hand, caught in the groove of a record with no discernible way out. Our responses had become habitual.

If we look at the work of Dr Bruce Lipton, he states, in his book *Biology of Belief*, that 'through the conditioned learning process, neural pathways between eliciting stimuli and behavioural responses become hardwired to ensure a repetitive pattern. Hardwired pathways are habits.'

He also states that 'Endowed with the ability to be self-reflective, the self-conscious mind is extremely powerful. It can observe any programmed behaviour we are engaged in, evaluate the behaviour and consciously decide to change the programme. We can actively choose how to respond to most environmental signals and whether we even want to respond at all. The conscious mind's capacity to override the subsconscious mind's preprogrammed behaviours is the foundation of free will.'

'However, our special gift comes with a special pitfall. While almost all organisms have to actually experience the stimuli of life first-hand, the human brain's ability to 'learn' perceptions is so advanced that we can actually acquire perceptions indirectly from teachers. Once we accept the perceptions of others as 'truths', their perceptions become hardwired into our own brains, becoming our 'truths'. Here's where the problem arises: what if our teacher's perceptions are inaccurate? In such cases, our brains are then downloaded with misperceptions. The subconscious mind is strictly a stimulus-response playback device; there is no 'ghost' in that part of the 'machine' to ponder the long-term consequences of the programmes we engage. The subconscious works only in the 'now'. Consequently, programmed misperceptions in our subconscious mind are not 'monitored' and will habitually engage us in inappropriate and limiting behaviours.'

Dr Lipton goes on to say that 'our responses to environmental stimuli are indeed controlled by our perceptions, but not all of our learnt perceptions are accurate. We do have the capacity to consciously evaluate our responses to environmental stimuli and change old responses any time we desire … and are not stuck with our genes or our self-defeating behaviours!'

The wonderful news from this cutting edge research is that we all have choices to continue in the same vein, yet we do have a choice to change. The choice is ours. We have free will. Just being aware of this can begin to support you in your transformation.

Anthony Robbins states that 'If you continue to do what you have always done, you will continue to get what you have always got.'

Looking at this in perspective it is important to understand that while you are taking this journey of self-discovery and awareness it is imperative to know that there is no blame to be apportioned to any part of yourself. When we begin to become aware of what is causing our stresses and anxieties, there is often a tendency to blame ourselves. This is something that needs to be avoided at all costs because the blame game is also a fear-based response, which will have a negative effect on your body chemistry. You are simply learning a new way of being. You are reprogramming those old habits, filling in the deep grooves on your record, to be eventually lifted up so that you can take a good look around the new vista that opens out before you. Take a moment to simply 'be'.

Develop an awareness of the moment in which you find yourself and become aware that everything in your world is a result of the choices that you make, as a result of what you believe. In this moment, know that you are right where you need to be, and that you can change anything about your life that you desire simply by choosing differently. Take the pressure off yourself; enjoy this journey of self-discovery and new way of viewing the world.

ACTIVITY

AWARENESS

For a few moments simply allow yourself to 'be'. Complete the breathing exercise from step stone I. Now start to become aware of what is taking place around you.

- What was happening around you?
- What emotion did you feel?
- Sit with those emotions for a few moments, allow yourself to experience them.
- Now think about a specific goal you have in life; what is it in your life you would like to change or achieve?

Make some notes about anything in particular that has arisen as a result of this exercise.

YOUR JOURNEY SO FAR:

- Your biography is not your destiny.
- You are free to make choices.
- Your health and wellness are affected by the choices you make; therefore it is important to be consciously aware of the choices you make, and to put these choices into perspective.
- The limiting beliefs you have about yourself are not true.
- Being aware and putting your world into perspective is a vital pathway towards health and wellness.

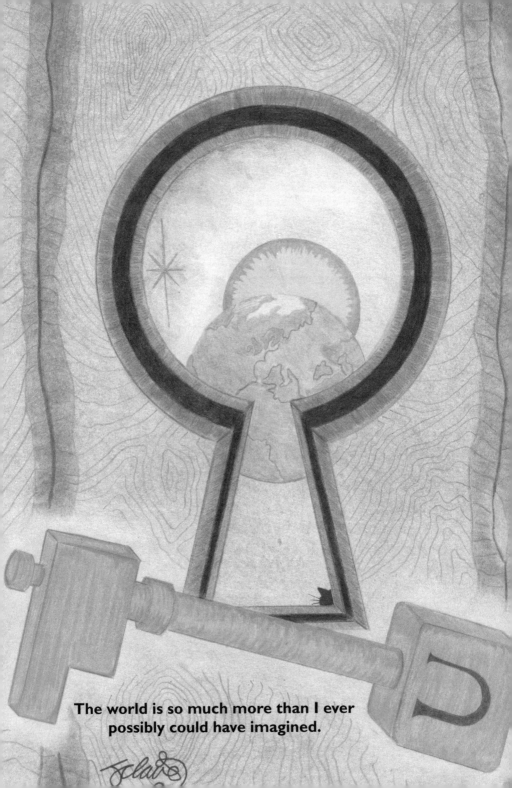

The world is so much more than I ever possibly could have imagined.

STEP STONE FOUR

THE GOLDEN KEY: THE ATOM AND VIBRATION

"Everything is made of light", he said, 'and the space between isn't empty".

Don Miguel Ruiz

On our own journey to wellness, we would not have been able to unlock our innate ability to reach our goal if we had not found the keys to unlock the deeper understanding of the world around us. Those keys were our release from the deep groove of negativity, despair and physical illness that we had trapped ourselves into – our habitual responses. As we became more aware of the choices we were making on a daily basis, we began to fill our deep, habitual groove with deeper understanding.

Our new perspective of the world helped us to view an open expanse of possibility that was laid out before us. From this point, our lives were never the same again. Moving beyond the awareness of our own habitual responses, we were introduced to deeper understanding, which supported our reconnection to wellness and the rediscovery of a nurturing, happy and healthy relationship with ourselves and everyone around us. In short, ancient, esoteric teachings met squarely and comfortably with quantum physics to help us to view life differently. We now wish to share these basic understandings with you in a philosophical context.

To obtain the most from this chapter, we feel that it would be helpful for you to spend some time with each concept before moving on to the next. Ensure you understand the information provided, really feeling the words within your body as best you can at this present moment in your development. Come back to this information as your development progresses in order to gain deeper understanding.

1. Energy: evidence from extensive research into subatomic physics tells us that there is no such thing as physical matter; everything is energy.

2. The atom: an atom is the smallest building block of matter (ie energy). Everything around us is made up of atoms, which contain neutrons, electrons and protons. The nucleus of the atom contains neutrons and protons, orbited by electrons. The nucleus is thousands of times smaller than the atom itself. For example, if an atom was the size of a football stadium, the nucleus would be comparable to the size of a pea. Whizzing some way out from the nucleus are the electrons, and between the electrons, the nucleus and the edge of the atom there are vast amounts of empty space. This means that nothing around us can be solid as most of the atom is empty. Therefore, how is it possible that we can sit down on something that we think is solid or even be holding this book? It is merely our beliefs and perception that create the world around us.

3. The quantum realm: from basic science we know that pretty much everything on Earth, in fact in the universe, is made of atoms. What we term solids, liquids and gases are the main states in which the atom exists. For the purpose of this explanation, take a look at everything around you in your environment now. The book you are reading, the chair you are sitting on, everything that surrounds you, even you. Then, imagine you have the world's most powerful microscope and that the whole environment in which you are sitting can be viewed underneath its lens. See that all of these things are dissolving into atoms. Scale down everything around you, imagining their smallest component parts (the atom). Perhaps you are imagining sparkling lights of resplendent colour, or little balls of atoms bumping into each other as they move about their business. Whatever you are imagining is perfect.

What this exercise shows, very simply, is that everything around you is now made up of atoms – you have changed your perspective. When you scale down those things around you into their smallest part, there is actually no chair, no book; nothing for you to label or identify. Everything surrounding you is exactly the same, made up entirely of atoms. Atoms that are almost totally empty space.

4. Vibration: all atoms vibrate. Therefore, we live in a universe made up of vibrating atoms. Dependent upon the speed of this vibration, known as frequency, the components such as sound, colour, light, matter and countless others are formed. The slower the speed of vibration, the denser this object is. Let us examine ice as an example. In water, the atoms within the liquid are vibrating at a specific speed; they contain a certain amount of energy, which maintains the water in its fluid state. If energy is taken away, reducing its vibration by placing it in a freezer; the heat will be taken away from the water and the atoms will slow down to the point where the water begins to freeze. If this process is reversed and the water is boiled, heat (more energy) is introduced to the water, down into the water molecules and the atoms. When heat is applied or reduced within an atom, energy is given or taken away, thereby increasing or decreasing the vibration, respectively. If the water is further heated, steam will be produced.

What this exercise shows is that the atoms in the water are merely vibrating at a higher or lower speed, which simply transforms the state into what we label as steam, water or ice. We will talk more about the topic of vibration in later chapters and why this is so important.

5. Intention and attention: energy (the atom) follows attention. For example, each radio station in the world is allotted a frequency for broadcast. When you want to listen to a specific radio station, you turn your energy (intention and attention) to the dial on your receiver and tune in to the station of your choice. When you do this and link into your chosen station, it does not mean that all other radio stations cease to broadcast. You are merely focusing your attention on a frequency that you are choosing to listen to. What this demonstrates is that energy follows attention.

6. What is real? Following this thought process, what becomes apparent is that what our five senses receive on a daily basis is merely our brain decoding these frequencies, producing images, sounds, smells and so on, that are familiar to us. Our eyes are purely lenses, and in themselves do not see. They process energetic frequencies given out by the objects that surround us, sending these frequencies to our brain to decode. These are then filtered through our personal belief patterns and cultural references.

To highlight this point, there is an ancient story that goes something like this: there was once an ancient tribe that looked out from the shores of their land and every day saw a ripple on the water. Thinking it was a large school of fish, they thought nothing of it and went about their daily business. Returning to the shoreline some days later, the tribe noticed that the ripples on the water were more pronounced, however they were not concerned and continued with their daily business. This continued for several more days, after which time the tribe began to feel uneasy, believing the ripples on the water to be a bad omen. One day, while in meditation, a medicine man from the tribe had a vision of a large wooden structure on the open ocean carrying with it foreign looking men. The structure was enormous and had poles with cloth that was emblazoned with strange and unfamiliar designs. Running down to the water's edge the medicine man drew in the sand what he had seen. At that moment the entire tribe looked out to sea and saw the ripples, yet now they also saw a large warship made from wood with billowing sails. This was exactly the vision that the medicine man had seen and drawn in the sand. Until that point, the tribe's people had no reference as to what a warship was and therefore could not 'see' it until it was too late.

In our eyes there are two types of light-sensitive cells, called rods and cones. They are both found in the retina, the layer at the back of the eye that processes images. Rods allow us to see in dim light or at night, whereas cones allow us to see in detail and distinguish colours. There are three types of cone cells: red, green and blue. Each cone has a different level of sensitivity to light. When we look at an object, light enters our eyes and stimulates the cone cells. Our brain then interprets the cone cells, allowing us to see the colour of the object. The red, green and blue cones all work together to allow us to see the whole spectrum of colours, for example when the red and green cones are stimulated to a certain level we see the colour yellow.

Colour blindness occurs when one or more of the cone types are faulty or missing. This means that someone who is colour blind has difficulty seeing the cone colour that is missing or faulty. For example, if the red cone is missing you will be unable to see colours containing red as clearly as others do. If individual people can interpret colours differently, then it stands to reason that each person will view everything around them differently, based on the multitude of filters that everyone has.

Finally, just because we can't see something doesn't mean it doesn't exist. We cannot see infra-red or ultra-violet rays at the extreme opposite ends of the visible colour spectrum, but they certainly exist and they have a measurable frequency. We also cannot see oxygen, however we know that it exists in our environment, because without it we would die.

7. Taking the pressure off: it follows that what we 'see' is purely based on our cultural references, our teachings and experiences. We learn and are taught what to see, and what not to see. One person's view of the world will always be completely different from another person's, therefore, we can never truly see another person's point of view. In this case, how can we possibly stand in judgement about what is right or wrong for another person? The answer is that we cannot because we are not them. We can only ever see our own view of the world, and we therefore realise that the only surety is the choices that we make ourselves.

8. Why are we here? Many ancient cultures believe that we incarnate on planet Earth to undergo experiences that occur as part of a contract that we made before we were born. We have therefore chosen our life, our parents, friends and experiences. When we move against our natural instincts or the experiences that we chose, we create a heavy energy vibration within our energy field because we are out of alignment with our purpose, we are out of alignment with our heart.

9. Karma: there are many views of karma. Karma basically means 'reaping what you sow'. In science this is translated into 'every action has a reaction'. Ancient people and many cultures today believe that we continue to reincarnate in a physical body to balance any karma that we may have accrued from previous lifetimes. The energy of what we did in other lifetimes is energetically stored somewhere within the universe and when we reincarnate this energy, our karma seeks us out. As we enter our teenage years, our karma finds us. When this happens, the heavy energy of this karma enters our energy field, resulting in negative, emotional feelings for what appears to be no apparent reason. This energy can be from many lifetimes ago, and can leave you feeling 'out of sorts'. There are also those who believe that there is no karma, and that life is to be experienced. This is perfectly valid, because each of us sees the world differently and energy follows intention. However, it is still important to acknowledge that whatever happens, science dictates that every action must have a reaction. Therefore, we have to be extremely careful about what energy we create in the first place, and think purely about creating from the heart.

10. Life after death? The laws of physics say that matter can neither be created nor destroyed. When we die and we leave our physical body isn't it possible that our soul takes our earthly experiences into another state? Our vehicle for our earthly incarnation is our body. Science has yet to locate where our thoughts, our consciousness, exist within the body. Our body is full of flesh, blood and bone, but what about our consciousness? Where does that reside? Might our thoughts, our consciousness, be part of our soul? These thoughts and consciousness are energies, that, when a physical body can no longer contain them, could well move out of the physical vehicle and away into another state. The laws of physics make this perfectly possible, and help to explain out-of-body experiences, ghosts, angels and the unexplained beyond the veil of this three-dimensional world 'reality'. The following story, taken from an article by Len Fisher, illustrates this point nicely. 'Weighing the soul' was the title of a project by an American physician called Duncan MacDougall, who carried out a series of experiments just over 100 years ago, based on the theory that if there were a soul it should weigh something. He placed beds containing dying patients on a large set of scales and watched for a sudden drop in weight at the moment of death. Several experiments gave him a figure of three-quarters of an ounce (about 21 grams). Modern scientists sniff at such a project, not least because they claim there are no rational grounds for believing that the soul exists. However, Fisher regards this as not exactly fair. While dismissing the soul, they are perfectly happy to believe in the existence of the Higgs boson, a particle that has never been detected or measured in any way, but which is currently the best explanation for a big scientific conundrum: why does anything weigh anything in the first place? Why does gravity act on the mass of an object to create weight? (Len Fisher, 2004, Weighing the soul – The evolution of scientific beliefs. Financial Times Online, accessed 02/02/2010.)

What these 10 points demonstrated to us was that the world that we had been educated to see around us, was merely an illusion, created by our cultural references, upbringing and programming. By beginning to implement this knowledge into our world, we began to understand that the world around us is created entirely by ourselves and therefore, we are responsible for what takes place within it. From selecting a radio station, to deciding whether to be happy or sad about a specific issue, it is simply us and not others who create the script that plays out around us. In other words, it is our choice how we react and whether we live with health and wellness, or in a state of fear and anxiety.

Another story, which we quote regularly, focuses on two individual people living separately on the same street. One person enjoys fantastic neighbours who can't do enough for him, yet the other finds his neighbours abhorrent and doesn't get on at all well with any of them. The neighbours haven't changed, they are exactly the same people, yet one person experiences a different view of the world, created entirely by themselves and their choices. By committing to bringing these deeper understandings of the world around you into your daily life, you can start to take the pressure off yourself and realise that you do have a choice about everything you experience in your life. The world around you starts to look different. No one outside of yourself is responsible for your lot in life, and while any decision that you make to change your situation will invariably not be easy, you do have the capacity to make choices and to change.

YOUR JOURNEY SO FAR:

- Your biography is not your destiny.
- You are free to make choices.
- Your health and wellness are affected by the choices you make; therefore it is important to be consciously aware of the choices you make, and to put these choices into perspective.
- The limiting beliefs you have about yourself are not true.
- You are an energetic being.
- Everything around you is made of energy.
- The physical matter that you perceive to be around you on a daily basis is merely energy vibrating at different speeds.

Everything is in
perfect balance.

'I think we each have a personal sweet spot as well. It's the state of mind in which we experience the most joy and satisfaction in being ourselves.

And from that place of pleasure and joy in being ourselves, energy arises to flow out into our day bringing with it the depth and resonance of our own beingness, bringing with it blessing.'

David Spangler

We now know that all energy is made in its purest form of vibrating atoms and subatomic particles, vibrating at different speeds (remember the water, ice, steam explanation in step stone 4?). As energetic beings, it stands to reason that we will be affected, on a daily basis, by the millions of energy patterns that swirl around us and within us, including mobile phone emissions, our own thoughts and the thoughts of others.

Yes, thoughts have an electrical frequency. The thoughts that we have on a second by second basis affect the chemical composition of our body on a second by second basis. Dr David Hamilton evidenced in his book *How Your Mind Can Heal Your Body* that our brain changes in relation to what we are thinking. In fact, our brain is changing every second of every day, just because of how and what we think.

Each brain cell, or neuron, is connected to another brain cell via what is called a neuroconnection. Interestingly, these neuroconnectors do not touch, and signals pass from one neuron to another via what is termed 'neuro-firing', or a bolt of electricity. So, our thoughts are being generated by a mini bolt of electricity each and every second of the day, generating energy and creating an energetic resonance or signature.

Everything that you think and feel determines your vibrational frequency. This frequency attracts to it other frequencies that harmonise (or resonate) with it – like attracting like. Therefore, if you are feeling stressed or angry, you will manifest a situation or person to you who is also stressed and angry. This is the basic law of attraction. Think about a room full of people laughing, somehow, you feel as though you want to join in. Laughter is, after all, contagious.

The law of attraction and like attracting like can at first glance seem like a contradiction; counter to what we learnt in basic science. However, both science and the law of attraction are on the same page.

As we discovered in step stone 4, everything in the universe is energy at the most basic level, and the current scientific consensus states this. We also know that everything in the universe vibrates.

Newtonian physics dictates that everything has an equal and opposite reaction. Science generally uses the terms negative or positive, however, for the purpose of this exercise it is helpful to understand them as masculine and feminine energies linking together to create. For example, masculine and feminine energies must combine to create a child. These same energies also combine to create a planet, a universe, even thoughts. This understanding works on all levels of creation and is the root of the law of attraction.

The popular film, *The Secret,* explains the concept of like attracting like very well and states that whatever you vibrate in harmony with is the masculine or feminine counterpart that will attract to you. If you are sending out a masculine vibration your energy will seek the feminine counterpart to create the experience you sent to the universe. Without the feminine, the masculine cannot create. Without the masculine, the feminine cannot create.

Clearly, if both energies do not vibrate in harmony with the other, they will not be attracted to each other. Like vibration attracts like vibration.

Think about the yin and yang symbol, which demonstrates beautifully how masculine and feminine energy work together. The symbol contains equal amounts of light and dark masses perfectly intertwined in a circle; a small dot of masculine imbued in the feminine, and a small dot of feminine imbued in the masculine.

The symbol is a sign of completeness; unity created by the other half of matter. This is the law of nature and the only way any single being or element can find completeness. The symbol represents these two energies constantly moving in cycles; night and day, hot and cold, life and death. The energies constantly balancing and rebalancing each other; the amount of energy never changing within the circle itself.

It is a perfect universe within its own right; an infinite dance of masculine and feminine energies. If either of these energies is not in harmony, they cannot coexist. Through this imagery we can see the concept of like attracting like, and subsequently the law of attraction at work. This law is not in conflict with science, we just need to explore it in more depth to truly understand it in its totality.

To illustrate this point, experiments have been carried out with violin strings. Two violins were placed at opposite ends of a room. The string on one violin was plucked, and after several minutes, the corresponding string on the unplucked violin at the opposite end of the room began to vibrate.

The reason this happens is because the plucked violin string begins to quiver, passing its resulting vibration and note in all directions into its environment, the air, the body of the violin and so on.

(Try closing your eyes and humming a note for a few seconds; did you feel the vibration in your mouth? Did the vibration extend anywhere else in your body? Did anyone else hear you?)

The molecules in the air nearest to the violin will be affected first by the vibration that has been produced by plucking the string. These molecules then bump into other molecules in all directions, eventually reaching the other side of the room where the second violin is placed. Because the molecules within the air are carrying a specific vibration, they will find resonance in the string that produces the corresponding note or frequency, therefore causing the violin string to vibrate without having been physically touched.

If we think about this law in terms of your health and wellness; whatever choice you make in terms of how you react to a specific situation will be having a direct impact on your physical and energetic body. So choosing to feel anxious or fearful will attract physical or emotional stress to you. Similarly, those feelings will also have an impact on everyone around you because of the frequency that you are vibrating at. There will be people who cannot stand to be around you because the frequency is too much for them and they do not resonate, in fact they are repelled. However, you will attract towards you those people who pick up and resonate on the same frequency.

Negative, fearful energy tends to be dense and heavy. This is also characterised in the words that people use to describe how they feel: 'I feel heavy of heart', 'I feel down/low', 'I feel under a cloud/in a dark mood'. These descriptions describe the dense and heavy energy of feeling low, of choosing the fear response.

Conversely, if you are feeling happy and joyful, you will resonate at a different frequency – lighter and brighter. This frequency promotes health and wellness within your energetic and physical bodies, and also magnetises people towards you who are also in that similar vibration.

We can clearly see the law of attraction, like attracting like, at work here. We manifest what we choose, what we focus our attention on. What follows, therefore, is that you are responsible for everything that occurs in your life because your vibrational frequency is set in place as a result of the choices that you make on a second by second basis.

It is important to understand at this point that it is OK to have a negative thought or feel down. We are not saying that you should deny your feelings. Simply be aware of what is taking place within your energy field on a moment by moment basis so that you can consciously do something about it.

As long as you understand the law of attraction and resonance, you will understand that whatever you feel will have an impact on yourself and others.

David Hamilton says that we should not be afraid of having a negative thought; simply that we should acknowledge any emotion that comes up, gently bringing them to the surface mindfully.

As a result of bringing these emotions to the surface, they have a better chance of exiting your system in a healthful way. As our body chemistry changes on a second by second basis, and consequently our body changes on a second by second basis, by the next day the original emotion will have changed into something else and you will have created a different physical and energetic structure.

Remember that research has shown that suppressed negative emotions are not good for us and left over long periods of time cause inflammation and dis-ease.

REFLECT

Take a moment to think about your own story; the journey through life you have made to this point. Can you think of a time when you attracted something into your life because of your vibrational frequency – your resonance? Was there a time when you were in a bad mood and everything in your day seemed to go wrong?

 Similarly, have there been people or experiences that you have been magnetised to in your life? If so, can you identify why?

YOUR JOURNEY SO FAR:

- Your biography is not your destiny.
- You are free to make choices.
- Your health and wellness are affected by the choices you make; therefore it is important to be consciously aware of the choices you make, and to put these choices into perspective.
- The limiting beliefs you have about yourself are not true.
- You are an energetic being.
- Everything around you is made of energy.
- The physical matter that you perceive to be around you on a daily basis is merely energy vibrating at different speeds.
- Your thoughts change your brain and affect the chemical composition of your body on a second by second basis.
- As a result of this, your energetic frequency attracts towards it circumstances and people who resonate with your exact frequency.
- We manifest in our lives what we choose to think and feel – energy follows attention.

I AM one with the universe,
and the universe is one with me.

MINDFULNESS AND SHIFTING INTO NEUTRAL

'Take the pressure off any situation by shifting into NEUTRAL – Non-judgement, Empathy, Unconditional love, Thoughtfulness, Respect, Acceptance, Light.'

Louise Claire-Pardoe and Jason Paul Claire

Mindfulness follows on from awareness. It is a philosophy, a way of viewing the world around us with concentrated attention on daily experiences from moment to moment.

It is a total shift from the current Western way of viewing the world, yet a practice that has deep implications for everyone, as the old ways of fear, stress and anxiety make way for a rediscovery of inner peace, health and wellness.

Mindfulness teaches us to pay deliberate attention to what is going on in our mind, body and day-to-day life, doing this with non-judgement, compassion, love and respect, both to ourselves and others. Integrating mindfulness into our daily lives can help us see things differently and move towards greater levels of health and wellness.

We discovered in earlier step stones that our thoughts change our brain and the chemical make up of our body. Therefore, when we are aware and mindful, it is possible to learn to view life differently and gently move towards greater levels of health and wellness.

We have used the philosophy of mindfulness successfully on ourselves and with our clients who have issues with anxiety, stress, addictions and long-term health conditions. Mindfulness teaches you to become more aware of your thoughts and feelings, and how these can affect physical, emotional and mental states of being.

Ancient people believed that life followed its own script, guided by higher levels of consciousness and not by the voice of the ego. They believed that they were spiritual beings incarnate on the Earth to undergo a human experience, part of a much bigger intelligent plan. Immersed in nature, they learnt from the environment, seeing that each living thing was totally interconnected.

The ancients lived in a way that connected them to the oneness of everything; the exact way that nature teaches us if we take the time out to observe it in full flow. They were totally and utterly aware of their state of being, allowing the natural laws of the universe to flow all around them and within them; never resisting, always flowing, even when surrounded by challenging circumstances. Even today, modern day shamans view life as a sacred journey, a journey of the soul that leads to wholeness.

From a place of fear and despair, we gradually learnt to view life more mindfully. Simply by allowing ourselves to shift our perspective on the world, we looked up at the stars and the cosmos above us, understanding in that moment that the universe beyond traversed billions of light years.

When we allowed ourselves to become aware and mindful of this, we knew that we were part of a much bigger reality and questioned why we were spending so much time fixating and worrying about smaller issues that we couldn't do anything about anyway. What we could do something about was how we reacted to the circumstances that were happening around us, by becoming more mindful, and subsequently calmer, happier and healthier, viewing life in a more rational and logical way.

We would like to share ten of the most profound principles that graced our life, which truly supported us to begin to live our lives more mindfully.

1. We are all made up of stardust. This has been proven scientifically, and therefore we are woven into the very fabric of the universe implicitly. Each one of us is a distillation of infinite oneness, of consciousness – each of us experiencing life in our own way.

2. These life experiences are unique to each one of us.

3. No one else can ever experience the world through our eyes. Similarly, we can never experience the world through their eyes.

4. We make our own choices, and as a result attract into our lives exactly what we need.

5. The only thing that we can change in life is our own reactions and our own actions.

6. You cannot be responsible for other people's reactions to you as they experience life in their way, influenced by their own layers of personal and socio-conditioning.

7. Your thoughts create the way you see the world; changing your thoughts will change your life by changing your script, as outlined previously.

8. Every action has a reaction. Therefore, what we give out we receive back.

9. The goal of life is to experience this incarnation in our own way. Some people will be mindful of karma, yet others will not; however, all people will be undergoing their own experiences.

10. Your natural state is wellness.

CHANGE OF PERSPECTIVE

In order to begin to work with the understanding presented above, and throughout this book, you may need a change of perspective on life beyond your current state of awareness. One way to help you open yourself up to this new information is to imagine that you are stuck in a room where you can only see the four walls, the ceiling and the floor. Are there adjoining rooms? To make an immediate judgement and rule out this possibility would be foolish; if you do not allow yourself to explore the possibility that there are other rooms surrounding you, you may be stuck in that room for the whole of eternity.

George Bernard Shaw said 'Progress is impossible without change, and those who cannot change their minds cannot change anything'.

As we realise that only we are responsible for our outer and inner world, the qualities of non-judgement, unconditional love, compassion and respect for all, including ourselves, become increasingly important. If each one of us is totally responsible for our own world, and we cannot see or experience what others do in theirs, what use is there in judging others for the choices that they make? How do we know what life experiences they have been through that make them act a certain way? What was their personal story that shaped them? We must accept that if we each have our own story, then others do too and we cannot begin to know what that story feels like to them because we are not them.

When we begin to accept ourselves for who we are, regardless of our baggage, we must therefore begin to accept others, regardless of theirs. This one, simple action immediately takes the pressure off us and those around us, because we experience life in our way, and others experience life in their way. Think about a time when you have stood in judgement on yourself or someone else – how did that feel? Chances are, not very good. If you didn't feel very good about it, you will have generated corresponding chemical reactions within your physical body, affecting your entire body chemistry.

However, in our Western world, we have become used to pointing the finger and judging others for the choices they make. Look at the world of celebrity, we devour gossip magazines with photographs of famous people carrying out simple day-to-day tasks; eating with their mouth open, having a wardrobe malfunction, going through relationship problems. Then we judge them as a result. However, how many times have we done similar things? Why is it one rule for one, and one rule for another? Standing in judgement on ourselves and others does not promote health and wellness, so let it go, and commit to your own health and wellness within your own world.

Why not, from now on, try introducing this simple action into your life to help you to rediscover health and wellness. Quite simply, if you resonate with someone, great! If you don't, move away with non-judgement and respect towards someone or something that does. What value does it serve to judge yourself or others? When we are in a loving, compassionate and respectful vibration for ourselves and others, we also generate lots of feel-good chemicals within our body, which lead us towards greater levels of health and wellness.

Remember, we choose how we affect our body chemistry for our continued health, or not.

We have discovered that the most effective way to achieve a life of health and wellness is to begin to look at life from a broader point of view, from a more spiritual viewpoint rather than from a left-brained, programmed mind. As you allow these timeless laws a place in your world, you may begin to notice subtle benefits of a life in alignment with the spirituality of our universe. You may begin to feel more peaceful and calm about the process of life, or be more ready to let things go, being mindful of the effect your choices have on your own health and wellness.

From a very young age our attention is focused on the physical world, with our beliefs, understanding and intelligence firmly rooted there. Almost all the challenges that arise in our lives are linked to the physical world, and because we believe this 'reality' we become lost totally within it. Within our physical world, we make the choice to become consumed by these problems, rather than seeing the problem from a higher viewpoint; detaching ourselves to take in the bigger picture. Rather than becoming immersed in our daily issues, if we had a bird's eye view our perspective would change and we could probably see a solution. Simply by viewing the world from a different angle, a different perspective, we could probably find solutions to our predicaments.

This exercise supports us in our move towards detachment, a way out of the perceived problem, moving towards not having the problem any more. If we allow our inherent spiritual nature to support us, our perception opens and leads towards a mind shift.

We discovered NEUTRAL when we were in the midst of difficult life circumstances. We were applying the previous step stones of awareness and mindfulness into our lives, supported by the ancient spiritual philosophies which we have shared with you, that helped us to gain some perspective on the situation. However, we were still feeling a little down, and were simply allowing our feelings to come to the surface so that we could acknowledge them and deal with them as appropriate.

One evening, we were talking about how lovely it would be if we could live our lives at a slower speed. How wonderful it would be to coast along in neutral for a while to give us a chance to put our new view of the world into perspective. At that moment we felt great inspiration and wrote down how living in neutral could support us as an acronym.

Non-judgement. By not judging ourselves and others we would take the pressure off ourselves emotionally. We realised that we were not responsible for how others reacted to us, so long as we always acted from the heart.

Empathy. We should always employ empathy towards ourselves and others to ensure that we remain within the heart space. Empathy ensures that we are not drawn into the drama of situations, merely that we acknowledge a situation from a point of detachment, making it easier to move beyond the feelings and reclaim health and wellness.

Unconditional love. Living in the heart space ensures that we are always plugged into unconditional love for ourselves and others. As we have learnt already, the energy of love creates harmony and wellness within our physical and energetic bodies.

Thoughtfulness. We realised that if we were thoughtful towards ourselves, we would create wellness within our physical and energetic body. In turn, we would radiate this feeling outwards to others, attracting like responses.

Respect. If we did not value ourselves and respect our place in the world, we would eventually attract negativity into our world. Respect is a gentle and loving energy, one which promotes wellness.

Acceptance. We cannot do anything about what life throws our way, but we do have a choice about how we react. Accepting what we can change and what we can't is acting within a state of mindfulness. From this point we can move into the type of response we wish to choose to maintain our health and wellness – love or fear.

Light. When we employed NEUTRAL in our lives fully, we started to feel happier and lighter. We envisaged the light and warmth of the sun energising our bodies.

If you want to, welcome this acronym into your life.

SHIFTING INTO NEUTRAL

For seven days, work through each of the seven letters, experiencing each characteristic of the letter in turn. On the first day, spend five minutes with N – non-judgement. Experience living your life without judging yourself or others; feel it, see it, hear it. How does that feel to you? Does that feel good? Work through each of the letters until on the seventh day you arrive at L – light. Experience golden light flooding through your body, through everyone in your life. How does that feel? Does it feel good?

As you feel these loving characteristics throughout your energy field, you will begin to change your body chemistry, radiating positive feelings into your environment, attracting similar energies into your life.

Make a note of all your experiences during the week.

YOUR JOURNEY SO FAR:

- Your biography is not your destiny.
- You are free to make choices.
- Your health and wellness are affected by the choices you make; therefore it is important to be consciously aware of the choices you make, and to put these choices into perspective.
- The limiting beliefs you have about yourself are not true.
- You are an energetic being.
- Everything around you is made of energy.
- The physical matter that you perceive to be around you on a daily basis is merely energy vibrating at different speeds.
- Your thoughts change your brain and affect the chemical composition of your body on a second by second basis.
- As a result of this, your energetic frequency attracts towards it circumstances and people who resonate with your exact frequency.
- We manifest in our lives what we choose to think and feel – energy follows attention.
- The state of mindfulness follows attention. Being mindful allows you to change your perspective of the world; you take the pressure off yourself and begin to allow yourself to live healthfully and happily.

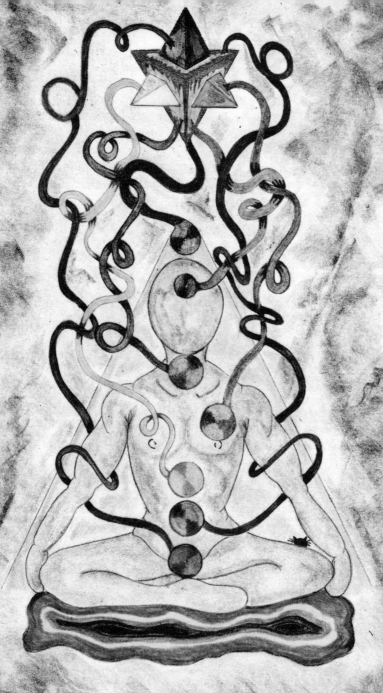

**I AM a spiritual being undertaking
a human experience.**

Vibration – 'Noun: an instance or the state of vibrating; informal: an emotional state or atmosphere, as communicated to and felt by others.'

Oxford English Dictionary

Before talking about the aura and chakras (what is termed the subtle energy system), it is important to reflect on what is meant by the term vibration. We discovered in earlier step stones, that atoms create energy by vibrating. Energy and matter are both forms of the same thing, vibrating at different speeds. From this perspective, we can see that everything that exists is a form of vibrating energy, including our physical bodies. Therefore, everything that surrounds us, colour, sound, light, words and the room you are sitting in, are simply different vibrational frequencies that your eyes see, your ears hear, and your brain decodes into images and sounds that are familiar to you.

Modern physicists have verified that we are all vibrating atomic and sub-atomic particles. Everything has a resonant frequency – the frequency at which it most naturally vibrates – from the chair that you are sitting on to this piece of paper. Every part, cell, molecule, gene and organ of your body also has a resonant frequency, as do all viruses and bacteria.

Just as atoms create energy, or frequencies, so the human body emits its own energy pattern because it is made up of atoms too. The functioning of the organs and all processes within our body generate heat and energy, which is emitted by the body into the space surrounding it. Today there is a great deal more acceptance that the body has its own energy system. Modern complementary therapy, for example, works directly with the aura and chakras, locating underlying energy imbalances that may eventually lead to physical problems. In modern complementary therapy practice, the person is seen as a complex interaction of different sorts of energy systems. Mind and body are not separated, for how can they be when we have learnt that everything is intimately connected? These energy frequencies may not be as apparent to the modern person as the physical body because we have been taught to not 'see' these energy systems. However, the systems themselves influence every aspect of our lives and they can be clearly felt by those trained to notice the changes they produce.

We have talked about the ancients, and it is well documented that ancient Indian seers perceived seven chakras; spinning vortices of energy running along the spinal column, each with its own responsibility for maintaining health. They developed exercises and meditations to help regulate and enhance the chakras to help promote wellness. The chakras represent the physical state of the body. A blocked chakra signifies dis-ease, whereas a balanced and clear chakra signifies wellness.

Think of the chakra system as the equivalent of a modern day motorway. A stream of cars (energy) move along the motorway, and at a motorway junction, several main roads move in from different directions to meet it. The motorway junctions represent the chakras of the body. The macrocosm always reflecting the microcosm, everything perfectly and intimately interconnected in a spiralling dance with each other. Everything around us in our external world, representing exactly what occurs within our inner world. Everything in a perfect relationship with everything else; never taking too much or too little, perfectly balanced.

When imbalance occurs, perhaps somebody driving too fast and close to the person in front, not being able to brake in time, or someone swinging out of their lane without looking, then an accident occurs. When the motorway becomes snarled up, the flow is blocked and the energy becomes dense and heavy. Something needs to be introduced to clear the blockage, which in our modern world would usually be the police or fire brigade. The blockage is cleared. In the same way, when our energy system becomes blocked, as a result of a fear response lodged somewhere within the body, disharmony occurs.

Everyone is unique and is likely to experience problems and energy stresses in different parts of the body and mind. Each specific chakra deals with particular areas of function, the quality of the energy varying from person to person. For example, a person experiencing work-related stress (created via a fear response) may develop a blockage in their solar plexus chakra. If left unchecked, this stress could manifest from the emotional body into the physical, presenting itself as digestive discomfort, for example irritable bowel syndrome. Another person may hold onto stress in the heart chakra, and if left untreated and unchecked, physical symptoms could manifest as angina or heart palpitations. Others might focus their stress or fear response in the third eye or crown chakra, and if left over a long period of time this could manifest into headaches or severe migraines.

It is understood that there are hundreds of chakras running through the human body, but the seven chakras that sit along the spinal column are treated as the main ones. Each chakra is associated with a specific characteristic.

1. Root: situated at the base of the spine, associated with survival instinct and grounding. This chakra governs the sexual/reproductive organs, tailbone, legs and feet.

2. Sacral: situated about 1in (2.5cm) below the navel, associated with emotions and sensuality. This chakra governs the ovaries, adrenal glands, spleen, uterus, urinary system, prostate gland, cervix and lower bowel.

3. Solar plexus: situated about 1in (2.5cm) above the navel, associated with personal energy and power. This chakra governs the pancreas, stomach, liver, small intestine, digestion and blood sugar.

4. Heart: situated in the centre of the chest, associated with love and relationships. This chakra governs the heart, lungs, thymus, blood, lymph and immune system.

5. Throat: situated at the throat, associated with communication and creativity. This chakra governs the neck, eyes, ears, voicebox, thyroid and sinuses.

6. Brow (or third eye): situated in the centre of the forehead, associated with intuition and insight. This chakra governs the pituitary, hypothalamus, eyes and autonomic nervous system.

7. Crown: situated at the top of the head, associated with knowledge and understanding. This chakra governs the pineal gland, hair, central nervous system and head.

In the first few step stones of this book, we presented our understanding and the scientific research that supports the fact that our choice of response to external influences has an immediate effect on the body. A response from love and acceptance creates a healthy heart rhythm and produces oxytocin in the brain. A response from a place of fear, by contrast, creates a frequency structure within the heart that is disordered and incoherent, upsetting the body's natural state of equilibrium. With the introduction of the chakra system, we can begin to pinpoint where exactly in the body would be affected by prolonged exposure to the fear response.

ACTIVITY

TUNING IN

Think about something in your life story over which you have chosen a fear response. Try to pinpoint where exactly that feeling is in your body. Make a note of this.

Now take a look at the information provided on the previous page concerning the chakras and the parts of the body they govern. You might find that the area you have pinpointed corresponds with a physical condition that you are experiencing.

This exercise helps you to become consciously aware of where exactly you store fear response feelings within your body.

Make a note of everything that happened for you as a result of this exercise.

As well as the chakras, all living things possess an electromagnetic field, popularly known as the aura. The aura is a measurable entity, because just as human beings generate heat through bodily processes, that heat must be able to be measured. Heat is energy and energy is created from atoms, which vibrate. Although many of us can't physically see the human aura, this doesn't mean to say that it doesn't exist. Just because we can't see infra-red and ultra-violet rays, doesn't mean to say that they don't exist.

It is said that the aura is made up of sheaths, each created from a finer substance or material from the one below it, rising from the densest to the lightest. The auric or energy body is a shield, sheath or energy layer and represents all aspects of the being. All emotions, thoughts and desires are reflected within the electromagnetic field. Darkened or weak colours identify areas that need cleansing and work. As we develop on our journey, it is vitally important to understand why it is necessary to keep our energy field protected, clean and vibrant in order to maintain good physical, emotional, mental and spiritual health.

From the physical world around us we can see that ice has a slow vibration, causing water to be solid. But the same material (water), when energy is given to it, increases its vibration and can become steam. Steam and ice are both made of water but the rate of vibration of both states is radically different.

Let us now look at our own body. If we are in an angry mood, this creates a heavy, dark vibration. We may often hear people talk about being in a 'dark mood'. As we have created this energy, it will vibrate within our energy field and if left long enough, will penetrate down from the energy field into the physical body. Some people are sensitive enough to pick up these subtle changes in energy and may ask you if there is anything wrong. Left for long periods of time, these heavy energies grow denser and denser, resulting in the energy field in that area becoming more and more blocked, until a point where physical illness can occur.

Conversely, if we find ourselves in a joyful and happy mood, we feel light. Energetically this produces a light vibration within our energy field. Lighter vibrations automatically connect us into love and acceptance, and generate a healthy energy flow around the body as we discovered earlier in this book.

So you can see how important it is to be aware of what is happening within your internal and external environments, as all of these things can have a profound effect on your energy field and your subsequent health and wellness.

The chakras and the aura show the physical and energetic health of the body. They can be affected not only by our own thoughts, but also by external influences. Below are some of the more common triggers for energetic imbalance in our modern world.

- Stress from a busy lifestyle.
- Physical toxins, such as processed food, alcohol or smoking.
- Energetic toxins, such as a negative environment, shouting or loud noises.
- Television, particularly dark, negative programmes.
- Demanding or energy-depleting people.
- Electricity pylons, mobile phones or artificial lighting.
- Lack of sleep and rest.

Prolonged exposure to any energetic imbalance will, over time, cause the body to become stressed. In physics, stress is defined as a force that causes strain on the physical body. Being stressed means different things to different people. Prolonged stress can cause burnout, leading to behavioural issues such as drinking, smoking, eating junk food, fatigue, insomnia or poor performance at work. Stress is also linked to heart disease, a weakened immune system (associated with a susceptibility to colds, and linked to rheumatoid arthritis), headaches, irritable bowel syndrome, cancer and mental health problems including anxiety and depression.

A person's susceptibility to stress can be affected by a multitude of factors, which means that everyone has a different tolerance to stressors. In respect of certain of these factors, stress susceptibility is not determined, therefore each person's stress tolerance level can change over time.

ACTIVITY

STRESS IN YOUR LIFE

1. Take a moment to identify what causes stress in your life.

2. When you are stressed, how do you feel? Where in your body do you feel it?

Make a note of anything significant that has arisen for you as a result of this exercise.

It is important to note that positive emotions will strengthen your physical and energetic body (your aura), bringing health, balance and vitality. Negative emotions, experienced over long periods of time, can manifest as sickness, instability, mood swings, low energy and damage not only to your physical being, but to your energetic body, your aura. This is the mind–body connection, a relationship that is key to your earthly health and wellness. Therefore, it is important to take stress seriously, as it is your body's way of telling you that it needs your support.

A simple way of supporting your energy field is to begin to integrate anything that makes you happy, that makes your heart sing, increasing the positive energy moving around your body. This can be done in many simple ways.

- Being with people that you love, such as friends or family.
- Being creative – painting or writing.
- Sitting in nature.
- Listening to relaxing music.
- Smiling and laughing.
- Eating fresh, nutritious food.

Remember that just as your own energy field can be heavy and dense, so can the energy field of those around you. This energy can be felt by sensitive people, and it is important to ensure that you are as protected as possible when walking around in this 'soup' of other people's energy every day. To recap what should be a familiar concept to you now, everything is made of atoms. Atoms are energy that emit a frequency. People around you will be emitting their thoughts and desires into the environment around them. As a matter of living our daily life, we come into contact with these frequencies and therefore need to be aware. Step stone 15 provides you with simple techniques to be able to protect and shield yourself on a daily basis. You might even find yourself feeling much better as a result of integrating these techniques into your daily life as well as knowing that you have a choice about how you react to external stimuli.

As you are now hopefully beginning to appreciate, any healing journey must involve some sort of shift, because it is true that problems of any kind cannot be solved from the place that created them. We have already talked in great depth about the fact that any journey to total health and wellness is not without its challenges, but the key to any healing journey and freedom is directly through the heart and unconditional love. For simplicity, in this step stone, we have introduced seven chakras to you, however, as we reach a fundamental stage in our planetary evolution we feel it would be helpful to say that there are a further five chakras that are becoming increasingly important at this stage in our evolutionary development. In her book, *The 8th Chakra*, Dr Jude Currivan says that 'the 8th chakra of the universal heart is the bridge between our ego-based perception and our higher awareness. On a collective level, we are now experiencing our resonance with this chakra as an increasingly global compassion'.

Dr Currivan continues, 'In accessing the universal heart, we transcend the limitations of our ego-based awareness and realize the multi-dimensional beings we really are. We also begin to comprehend the purpose of our soul'.

We will discus this in more depth in our next book, but Dr Currivan's words are extremely pertinent at this stage as we must understand that we do not undertake the healing journey merely for ourselves. More importantly, our commitment to our own healing journey, directly and positively affects the collective whole, as we realise everything is intimately and perfectly interconnected – the macrocosm reflecting the microcosm and vice versa. From the space of the universal heart, each one of us can harness the ability to not only heal ourselves, but everything and everyone else within the entire universe.

In her book, Dr Jude Currivan says 'In the commonality of our divinity, we are all ordinary. In the commonality of our divinity, we are all extraordinary'.

YOUR JOURNEY SO FAR:

- Your biography is not your destiny.
- You are free to make choices.
- Your health and wellness are affected by the choices you make; therefore it is important to be consciously aware of the choices you make, and to put these choices into perspective.
- The limiting beliefs you have about yourself are not true.
- You are an energetic being.
- Everything around you is made of energy.
- The physical matter that you perceive to be around you on a daily basis is merely energy vibrating at different speeds.
- Your thoughts change your brain and affect the chemical composition of your body on a second by second basis.
- As a result of this, your energetic frequency attracts towards it circumstances and people who resonate with your exact frequency.
- We manifest in our lives what we choose to think and feel – energy follows attention.
- The state of mindfulness follows attention. Being mindful allows you to change your perspective of the world; you take the pressure off yourself and begin to allow yourself to live healthfully and happily.
- The chakras and aura show your physical and energetic health. Be mindful of your own thoughts and external influences that can affect these in both positive and negative ways as they affect your health and wellness.

I choose to listen to
my inner voice, the
part of me that knows
what is best.

'The only journey is the journey within.'

Rainer Maria Rilke

The ultimate solution to all of the issues within our lives lies somewhere within ourselves.

As you discovered in the exercise where you shrunk yourself and everything around you down into atoms (in step stone 4), we are all fundamentally connected to everyone and everything that has been, is and ever will be, because we are all made of the same stuff. Therefore, how can we not have access to all the answers and knowledge that we could ever possibly need within ourselves?

In the West, the majority of the population has been educated from a very early age in the 'truths' of the modern world. One of these fundamental truths is the belief that there is separation; the separation of mind from spirit, the body from the mind. If this belief continues to be accepted, it is not surprising that people will lose connection with themselves, their inner voice, their gut instinct.

Instinct is described as an inborn pattern of behaviour that is characteristic of a species, often a response to specific environmental stimuli. Think about nature for a moment and the spawning instinct in salmon or the pack instinct of wolves.

Now turn your attention to primitive man kneeling at a watering hole taking a drink. As primitive man, our attention would be extended out around us to ensure that we weren't taken unaware by any predators who would view us as a tasty meal. We therefore had to develop a strong instinct, a gut instinct or sixth sense, to ensure that we were not attacked.

Over time, our sixth sense or gut instinct has been sidelined and dismissed by society to be replaced by the ego, the part of us that looks after basic needs, survival and protection. It is important to note that when balanced, the ego lives in perfect harmony with our instincts. We need the ego as it is also another part of us that keeps us safe. Interestingly, our modern day world is totally geared to strengthen the ego, causing it to become unbalanced and out of alignment with our being. When this happens, we make decisions not from a place of true knowing and instinct, but from an unbalanced ego, placing us in a position of fear or self-importance.

However, our natural instinct is one of the most important and inherent skills that each and every single one of us possesses. True instinct is generated not from the ego, but from the soul, the part of us that is always in connection with everything around it. The ego, on the other hand, can foster a sense of separation. It wants to keep us safe, even if it causes untold grief if it is unbalanced. By viewing external cues and labelling them as harmful or good, the ego, when left to its own devices, is happy to isolate us from the world, compounding the detrimental effects that it once sought to guard us from.

Is it our instinct talking or is it our ego? The ego, or id, tends to act according to what brings us pleasure, seeking to avoid pain or harm and generally keeping us safe. It is firmly based in our primitive fears of safety, protection and survival. Yet, sometimes, we just know that we need to quieten the ego and follow our inner voice. The trouble is, many of us have learnt to ignore our gut instinct in favour of the unbalanced ego part of us, which we believe keeps us safe – yet this is far from the truth. Keeping us safe has always been of paramount importance to the ego, but for many, it is now out of control. The more we try to ignore the ego, the louder it shouts, because over time it has been allowed to run free.

What follows is a perfect example of disharmony between a quiet instinct and a very noisy ego.

We both knew instinctively that we should have left our respective posts at work to set up our own business a long time before we actually did. Events at work were becoming more challenging; working in the environment we found ourselves in did not make us happy. We knew that we should leave, but the world in which we existed said that we had to work hard, pay a mortgage and save for a rainy day. The ego asked, how could we do this if we left our security behind? What were the guarantees? Even though we were very unhappy and becoming physically unwell, our unbalanced egos (fed entirely by the fears of the modern world) did not want change, and in order to 'protect' us kept us in jobs that were detrimental to our overall health and wellness. Our unbalanced, fear-based egos were happy to keep us in this position because the unknown is a very scary place for the ego to exist. The unknown simply being, what would happen if we left work and tried something new – something that our true, gut instinct had been trying to help us to see for many years. Unfortunately, the world in which we existed fully supported the ego and the ego fully supported the world in which we lived. It drowned out our inner voice, our gut instinct, to such a point that we could not hear it. We knew that something had to change, but for over four years each of us stayed in a position that we should have left a long time before. In the end, our egos were exhausted, we were physically and mentally unwell, at which time the egos let go and made way for our instincts to speak.

This chapter is not written to vilify the ego, but to impress upon you that everything needs to work together in harmony, in balance; the ego working in perfect harmony with our instinct, the head working in harmony with the heart. As with nature and the yin–yang symbol; everything functioning perfectly together.

At this point on your journey you will now be more consciously aware of the choices that you are making on a daily basis. You will begin to realise how the world around us is currently set up to disarm us of our innate ability to know exactly what is right for us; thereby giving our power away.

ACTIVITY
DO YOU LISTEN TO YOUR INSTINCT?

Think about a significant event from your life story. Did you make a choice that went against your initial instinct? If so, what did you know to be true at the time?

Can you pinpoint any other times within your life when you acted contrary to your gut instinct?

Do you always seem to fall into the same pattern of response?

Make notes of anything significant that has arisen as a result of this exercise.

We may call our instinct by numerous different terms:

- Gut instinct
- Higher self
- Inner voice
- Inner knowing
- Sixth sense
- Our soul.

Each of these terms means different things to different people, based on their own view of the world. Where the instinct exists may also vary in different people. Some people might say the head, others the heart, others the stomach or the gut. Other people may say that it is all around them, like consciousness. Wherever your instinct is situated for you is OK, because that is exactly where it is. What is important now is to reconnect with it, if you feel you have lost contact, welcoming it back into your life with love and gratitude.

ACTIVITY

CONNECT TO YOUR INSTINCT

Find a place where you will not be disturbed and make yourself warm and comfortable. Close your eyes, both feet on the floor, hands comfortably in your lap. Steady your breathing, taking deep, cleansing breaths in and out, relaxing with each exhalation.

Now tune in; ask your physical and energetic body where your instinct is situated. Feel, see or know where it is; whatever comes to mind is right.

When you are connected to your instinct, thank it for always working with you and welcome it back into your life with a smile. What is it saying to you?

When you are finished, take three deep breaths, allowing the image of your instinct to fade away as you bring yourself back to this time and space. You may wish to conduct this exercise regularly in order to re-establish a stronger relationship with your instinct.

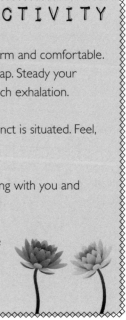

Reconnecting to your instinct will help you, over time, to become more trusting of it as you re-learn how it operates and that it never guides you wrong. We all generally know what would be best to do in a given situation, yet we often allow the ego to take over, placing obstacles and 'yes, buts' in the way. When in the natural flow, our instinct guides us through life, supporting us to achieve exactly what we need to achieve, keeping us on our life path. Some might say it is the conductor of our life script. When we have outgrown a situation, our instinct tells us to move on, yet how many times have we made things hard for ourselves by staying? How many times has our physical or emotional health suffered as a result of contravening our natural instincts?

By shifting your perspective and allowing your instinct to speak, you are perfectly placed to understand the fundamental truths that everything within our universe is intimately and perfectly connected, a cosmic dance of balanced energies. Anything that disconnects us from this natural state, our birthright, is merely an energetic illusion. Our instinct is totally inherent within us, yet it is mysterious and unfathomable, discoverable yet undiscoverable and known yet unknown. We can't really explain it logically, yet how is it that we simply know when we should or shouldn't do something? The feeling we experience generally turns out to absolutely right. If we have ignored it, many of us can recall instances when we totally regretted that choice.

While we may not be able to explain it logically, there is no denying that the instinct exists. As we have said many times before in this book, just because we can't explain it, or locate it scientifically, doesn't mean to say that it doesn't exist.

Thinking back to the beginning of this step stone, how is it that salmon know exactly where to return to spawn? It is totally inherent within them and they return to the exact same stream after many years away. Science has tried to explain why this is the case, citing numerous possible explanations, including the use of chemical cues, water currents and a variety of other senses to guide them back to the place where they were born.

We firmly believe that the instinct is the bridge between the logical, explainable world and the world of the ancients, where anything is possible and true manifestation can be created. It is our portal to the inner and the outer worlds; interconnected worlds where instinct, sixth sense and oneness are perfectly possible, and better still, perfectly explainable.

The instinct shows us a realm beyond the logical, beyond the 'seen' and the five senses. Simply by changing our view of the world and by the choices that we make, we can truly bring forth unlimited abundance and satisfaction because the universe is plentiful and abundant. If the universe is full of abundance, and we are totally connected to everything within it, all we have to do is manifest it, simply by our thoughts, ensuring they are always aligned through the moderator that is the heart. We have never been separated from the silent watcher at the heart of consciousness; we cannot possibly be. There is no duality. It is only by our own free will that we have moved from oneness and created what we think is the reality of the world around us. We can change it back, just by our own free will – by choice.

This is one route to reconnecting to, and creating, your birthright of health and wellness. Realising that we are all connected to source energy, we are all one with oneness, and as a result, we are everything and everyone around us.

As we have discovered, the evidence from extensive research into subatomic physics tells us that there is no such thing as physical matter. Everything is energy. All energy vibrates; you are energy, therefore you vibrate. Everything vibrates, even thoughts, so negative thoughts create negative vibrations, and positive thoughts, positive ones. All of this affects your energy system (your spiritual, physical, mental and emotional bodies). Now apply this principle to everything in your life, your thoughts, your daily interactions with people, what you watch on the TV and what you read in the newspaper. Daily life is a roller-coaster of emotions.

When we realise this, we understand that no one else outside of ourselves is creating our world. We have to take total responsibility for everything that happens within our lives, and if we do not resonate with something, we have the power to change it. There is nothing or no one outside of ourselves that can take the blame.

As newborn babies, we have no filtering system, no preprogrammed beliefs, and left in our own little world, our brain learns to 'see' what is actually around us – energy patterns, vibratory frequencies of light and dark. We have all watched young babies looking into a seemingly empty room intently watching something, yet at that age they have no preconceived ideas or understanding, and as a result, are totally open to what is around them.

Those young children who see discarnate entities, or who are lucky enough to have parents or guardians who are open to these ideas, encourage the young child and over time they learn to see and interpret the energy patterns that are around them, without fear of judgement or ridicule.

Those who do not, are told that it is simply their imagination and to stop being so silly. Without a place to feel safe, these children programme themselves to stop seeing what cannot be explained in our modern day culture, never to speak about it again. Yet our imagination is just as important as our instinct; some might say they are intertwined. Even Albert Einstein said 'Imagination is more important than knowledge'. Through his own imagination he was inspired to put forward his famous theory about the speed of light, after imagining himself travelling through space on a beam of light.

It has also been proved that our brains are unable to distinguish between what is 'real' and what is 'imagination', as Dr David Hamilton states in his book *Your Mind Can Heal Your Body*. There is a great deal of research occurring in this area, one study in particular encourages a disorganised person to visualise/imagine themselves being ultra-efficient and getting things done for seven days.

Following this time, new neural pathways will have been created in that person's brain, implanting the subconscious belief that they are efficient and get things done. Given that we now know that energy follows intention/attention, the odds are that the person is probably acting more efficiently and is completing more tasks than they ever did before.

Over time, our brain is programmed to see separation through parental teachings, our culture and belief patterns. The energy waves that are always so distinctly all around us and within us are eventually decoded by our brains, through the filter system of our beliefs and emotions, as totally separate to us – another human being, an animal, a plant, a tree, the sky, Moon and planets.

As we grow older and become part of society, we lose the innate ability to decode the essence/energy of that which we are observing, until our field of vision is narrowed to a tiny frequency of energy and light. Narrowed by the teachings we have received, our beliefs, our culture and fear of being different. We lose this inherent ability, the instinctive part of our nature that keeps us on our life path, that tells us when we need to be making changes.

However, we are at a point in our human evolution where we can no longer deny scientifically that which the ancient tribes of the world have always known. That there is no separation and our instinct is an inherent part of each and every one of us.

By becoming mindful and aware of connecting with your instinct, you allow yourself to open to a truth you have always known, and remember who you truly are. You are a magnificent being, more than your physical body, whose birthright is one of health and wellness.

YOUR JOURNEY SO FAR:

- Your biography is not your destiny.
- You are free to make choices.
- Your health and wellness are affected by the choices you make; therefore it is important to be consciously aware of the choices you make, and to put these choices into perspective.
- The limiting beliefs you have about yourself are not true.
- You are an energetic being.
- Everything around you is made of energy.
- The physical matter that you perceive to be around you on a daily basis is merely energy vibrating at different speeds.
- Your thoughts change your brain and affect the chemical composition of your body on a second by second basis.
- As a result of this, your energetic frequency attracts towards it circumstances and people who resonate with your exact frequency.
- We manifest in our lives what we choose to think and feel – energy follows attention.
- The state of mindfulness follows attention. Being mindful allows you to change your perspective of the world; you take the pressure off yourself and begin to allow yourself to live healthfully and happily.
- The chakras and aura show your physical and energetic health. Be mindful of your own thoughts and the external influences that can affect these, in both positive and negative ways, as they affect your health and wellness.
- Your instinct is real and guides you safely through life.
- The ancients taught that we are so much more than our physical experience.
- You are part of everyone and everything; within you lies the reflection of the entire universe, and therefore consciousness and its latent and infinite potential lies within you.

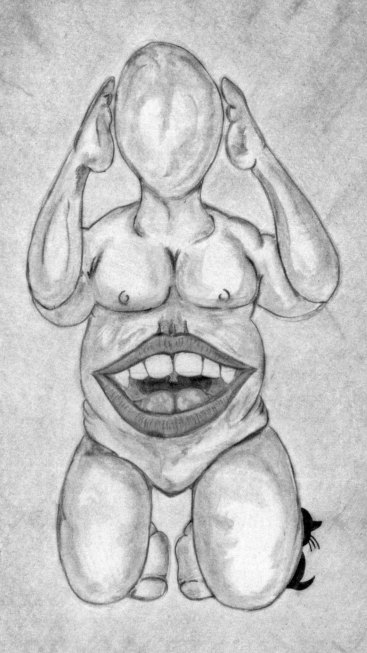

My body is always talking to me; by listening
to it I reconnect to health and wellness.

'You can live a life of fear, or live a life of love. You have the choice!

But I can tell you that if you choose to see a world of love, your body will respond by growing in health.

If you choose to believe that you live in a dark world full of fear, your body's health will be compromised as you physiologically close yourself down in a protection response.'

Bruce Lipton PhD

By becoming aware and mindful of the choices that you make in your world and connecting to your inner guidance, as demonstrated in step stone 8, you will find that your body is always talking to you, as a result of the universe talking to it, ensuring that it is kept on track.

LISTENING IN

Before we go any further, try listening in to your body and get a feel for what it is telling you. Close your eyes, take some deep breaths and become mindful of what is happening. Listen in to your body; welcome it as a friend into your awareness.

Are there any sensations in your body? If so, how would you describe them? Where in the body are they?

What might these be in relation to?

This exercise helps you to begin to listen to your body and deepen your awareness of the world around you. Listening in to its natural ebbs and flows, determining whether there is anything happening that you need to be aware of. The reason for this is that our body is a natural antenna. Each second of every day we are receiving millions of bits of information from the universe.

As we have learnt previously, our conscious mind can only be aware of seven (plus or minus two) pieces of information at any given moment. Everything else gets stored into our subconscious mind. Because we live such busy, fast-paced lives within this information age, we find that subtle indicators from the universe are ignored by our filtering system in favour of unbalanced ego-related issues. These subtle indictors are designed to help keep us on our life path and can come in many forms, including moments of synchronicity, coincidence or feelings.

Moving beyond the modern day world of separation, which we now know to be an illusion, there exists a world where everything that happens around us is part of a bigger plan, part of a cosmic dance where everything is completely and inherently linked. It is said that there are no accidents, that everything we experience is by design and what we subsequently attract into our physical world.

Synchronicity, or coincidence, has been described as patterns that repeat in time, possibly two or three times, causally unrelated, yet occurring together in a way that creates meaning to the observer. The more consciously aware you become, the lighter your energetic frequency becomes and you begin to attract more incidents of synchronicity into your life. As you become more consciously aware, what you focus on begins to manifest towards you, and you begin to find that the universe is talking to you on a second by second basis, guiding you and keeping you safely on your path.

While you may not yet be aware of synchronicities within your life, or you may be dismissing them altogether as not real, there are indeed many other ways that the universe communicates with you. Feelings, images, smells and sounds are all methods of communication and were greatly revered by ancient peoples.

Let us consider for a moment a woman who is in a toxic relationship with her partner. She is deeply unhappy, feeling emotional and finding it hard to sleep at night. There seems to be no way out, so the best thing to do is to just 'put up, and shut up' although deep within her soul she knows that she should leave. Another year on, the woman hoped that things would improve but, inevitably, they have become worse and she is now having to cope with regular violent outbursts from her partner. Daily life is now unbearable, her work is suffering, and physically she has started to manifest panic attacks, which leave her short of breath and suffering with palpitations.

The woman instinctively knew a long time ago that she should leave this toxic relationship, yet she stayed out of fear, firmly based in the ego mind. The best action she could have taken to preserve her overall wellness would have been to escape and move away. While this could have proved difficult, generally she would have been listening to the universe's direction and her inner guidance, ultimately preserving her overall health and wellness.

A year on, however, the universe and her body are having to shout even louder because she is not listening. Her home situation has become worse and turned violent, the universe throwing even more at her, forcing her to make the decision best for her highest good, but still she stays. So her body takes even more of a pounding and she manifests severe panic attacks.

Both the universe and her body are screaming out to her to listen. She knows what she should do, yet something still stands in the way.

We are not saying that these decisions are easy; sometimes it is better to cope with the devil you know. Yet, the universe only wants what is best for us, and we know deep down that our natural state of being is one of health and wellness. So if we know this, what is keeping us chained to our bar-less prison?

When we listen to the universe and our body, and commit to making changes for our highest good, the universe always supports us. We just have to trust that everything will be OK, and allow ourselves to be supported. We cannot know of all the infinite possibilities that the universe can send our way to help us achieve health and wellness.

All we need to do is to let go and trust that everything will be OK, because as we commit to becoming aware and mindful, and commit to listening to everything that happens within us and around us, the universe sees this and supports us.

ACTIVITY

MOVING ON

Think about something in your life that causes a negative sensation in your body; something you may wish to change, it could be a limiting belief or anything else that you have identified as part of your life story. Take your time and allow yourself to answer the last two questions truthfully. This is vitally important to find out if you are ready to move on.

Where in the body are you feeling it?

What are you feeling? (Emotions, thoughts, sensations)

What does that look like? (Colour, shape)

What is it attributed to? What is the trigger?

Do you need this?

How is this serving you; what benefit is it giving you?

The questions 'Do you need this?' and 'How is this serving you; what benefit is it giving you?' are probably two of the most important questions you will ever ask yourself.

As we know, there are only two basic emotions in the human psyche that direct our actions – love and fear. Any action that we take, like answering a question, will consequently be derived from one of these places, as a result of our experiences to date, our limiting beliefs and so on. Choosing love ensures that we are firmly in a place of connection, of health and wellness. Choosing from a place of fear unbalances us and upsets our natural equilibrium. Remember, in the activity above we asked you to answer truthfully. Truth is always derived from a place of love, from the heart. Yet often our ego minds tell us what the 'truth' is, when really it couldn't be further away from the truth for our health and wellness.

Let's talk for a moment about when we knew in our hearts that we should leave our well paid, secure jobs and become self-employed. Our bodies were telling us, Louise's more loudly, that we should leave. In the end, our bodies were screaming at us to listen. Our egos, on the other hand, were saying 'Another year, just stay for another year, that will give you enough time to save up some money to support you with the transition'.

However, another year on, we were still in jobs that were unfulfilling and weren't aligned with what our hearts knew we should be doing. Our hearts and minds were in total disharmony; physically and emotionally our health began to suffer even more. When we asked ourselves what benefit feeling this way was giving us and how this was serving us, we answered with the 'truth' of the ego. 'It'll be fine, just one more year. The benefit of saving more money far outweighs the detrimental health effects.'

Our limiting beliefs and ego-fears about our security and where our income would come from were more important to our ego than our health. In the end, our health bit back and we were forced to leave our jobs and take time out to recuperate. Now we are totally in alignment with our hearts and work for ourselves doing a job we love; our egos are balanced, we continue to pay our bills and we live in a world of health and wellness.

How we look back and laugh now. If we had answered directly from the heart we would have known that our health and wellness were not being served at all in a positive way, and we would have made a decision to leave much sooner.

We have already talked at length about the unbalanced, fear-driven ego that many of us possess. Often answering truthfully, from the heart, can cause great fear and panic for the ego, which simply wants to pigeon-hole us and keep us in a familiar place, even if this is detrimental to our health and wellness. However, we know that when we operate from the heart, we reconnect to universal consciousness and we are steered perfectly on our path, everything falling into place around us like a jigsaw puzzle.

As the wise man says, 'If something isn't working any more, change it'.

Therefore, when we answer any significantly important question about why we are not progressing in life or why we are unable to change, we ultimately find ourselves trapped in this dichotomy between the ego and the heart.

When you view any situation in your life, it must be through the eyes of the heart, firmly based in the response of love. While no one said that this, or the consequences, would be easy, this is the best way to reconnect to your path and rediscover your health and wellness.

Let's try the exercise again.

ACTIVITY

MOVING ON

Close your eyes, breathe deeply and link directly into your heart. Feel it fill up with warmth. Remain in the heart space for the duration of this exercise.

Think about something in your life that causes a negative sensation in your body; something you may wish to change, it could be a limiting belief or anything else that you have identified as part of your life story. Take your time and allow yourself to answer the last two questions truthfully, through your heart. This is vitally important to find out if you are ready to move on.

Where in the body are you feeling it?

What are you feeling? (Emotions, thoughts, sensations)

What does that look like? (Colour, shape)

What is it attributed to? What is the trigger?

Do you need this?

How is this serving you; what benefit is it giving you?

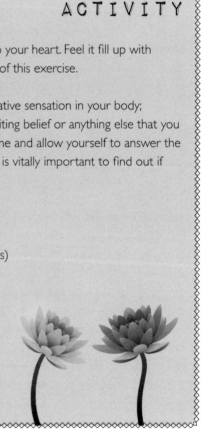

Were your answers to the last two questions different this time around? Make a note.

Perhaps you have identified that your ego-fear is still guiding your choices and actions?

However, as you learn to listen to, and trust, your heart wisdom, you realise that this is the only true pathway to overall health and wellness.

As we said earlier, the first step in changing anything within your life is to become aware. We are now taking this concept deeper, beginning to show you how to become reacquainted with your body; talking and listening to your body as a dear friend. It is your vehicle for your physical incarnation, and it is always talking to you, but the chances are that you have not really been paying attention until now.

From this point onwards, commit to talking and listening to your body as your friend. As your body is intricately connected into the natural ebbs and flows of the universe, from the heart space it will always guide you perfectly along your journey in life. Sometimes we are unable to see what the outcome might be. We just need to trust, let go and know that everything is perfect. (We discuss these concepts in more detail in later step stones.)

So from now on, commit to stop rejecting parts of yourself that you do not like. From the heart space, allow emotions to come up, recognising and experiencing them as they do so, because stuffing them down leads to disharmony. When you are ready, let them go and choose an action that leads to your health and wellness.

Becoming aware of patterns

When I (Louise) was a young girl, I remember playing in the garden on a beautiful summer's day wearing a lovely purple and blue dress adorned with pictures of bright flowers. I recall standing in total fear as a big bumble bee slowly buzzed up to me and landed on one of the flowers on my dress, thinking that it was a real flower. Petrified, I remember screaming at the top of my voice and running around the garden as fast as my little legs would carry me, with a rather bemused bee holding onto his 'flower' for grim death.

After that incident, I carried an irrational fear of bees through life, closely followed by a fear of anything that buzzed or was small and insect-like and flew. I had associated the bee with fear and while I can now sit in my garden on a beautiful summer's day and be comfortable with our natural habitat, I sometimes come out in a cold sweat if one of my winged friends unexpectedly comes a little too close.

Patterning is often created through our experiences. I associated the bee with danger and fear, connecting directly into my fight or flight instinct. I then developed a belief that all bees were dangerous, followed closely by wasps, flies, dragonflies and so on. Left to its own devices, my limiting belief led me to a stage in life where I hated the summer and wouldn't go out for fear of getting stung. And, when I did venture out, what happened? Yes, you're way ahead of me – I got stung. Remember, energy following attention/intention.

My fear-based belief about our winged friends was totally irrational and illogical. The bee didn't sting me when it landed on my dress, it merely came to say hello and try to obtain some pollen from my printed flower. However, my ego interpreted the situation as something quite different. The belief, meme or virus successfully replicating, infiltrating and spreading.

From what we have learnt about resonance and vibration in earlier chapters, it follows that all aspects of health and wellness are intimately linked to our energetic frequencies, which are directly linked to our choices of response (love or fear), as a result of external stimuli or triggers. For example, many people who suffer with an illness are programmed to constantly tune into the illness channel 24/7, thus maintaining this frequency and prolonging suffering. These fear responses can become habitual. Over time, we know of no other way to react, so we continue doing the same thing, regardless of whether this is beneficial for our health and wellness or not.

It follows that if you tune into BBC Radio Four, you will hear talking on the radio not opera. If you dial your sister on your mobile phone in Scotland, you will not get your friend Michael in the USA. We know that energy follows attention. For many years, I (Louise) was constantly plugged into feeling fear about my health and worrying about whether my heart would let me down again, to the point where I chose to become agoraphobic. My responses had become habitual, choices made out of fear, and I was stuck in a repetitive pattern.

As we now know, if your energy is vibrating at a low frequency and you are feeling the fear response, it follows that your body will not be working as efficiently as it could be.

You may find you have trouble concentrating or remembering things. This energetic imbalance within your system can eventually cause physical, mental or emotional problems. If your physical energy is blocked or sluggish and is left for prolonged periods of time, aches and pains including headaches, irritable bowel syndrome and other symptoms become commonplace.

Heavy and dense frequencies (energy) of fear and anxiety produce poor health. High frequencies of love and joy produce good health. If you commit to changing and improving your energetic frequency, through becoming aware of the choices that you make, it follows that over time you will feel better and live more healthfully.

Very often we find ourselves caught in patterns within life, perhaps we keep getting ill, or manifesting angry people around us. We need to become aware of these patterns, then discover what part of the body is affected as a result and how that feels to us, then commit to understanding why or what this pattern is associated with. What is the trigger?

From this point of understanding, a choice can be made as to whether you step off the wheel, or whether the pattern continues. Remember, the body is always trying to tell us something as a result of what is happening around it. While some triggers are small, others can be quite traumatic, and it is helpful to realise when you may need additional support to help you work through some of the issues that you have identified as a result of working through this book. Perhaps consider visiting a counsellor, holistic therapist or support group (a list of useful resources is given at the end of the book) while you continue with your development.

Making choices as a result of external stimuli or triggers, has an immediate effect on our health and wellness. Over time, this patterning can become habitual. However, it is possible to change these patterns, and to change what manifests within our daily reality. Because this topic is so big, we have limited space to cover material in depth here. You will have read in earlier step stones some key evidence from mind–body researchers around the globe who have looked deeply into the mind–body connection. If you would like to carry out more reading around this massive and fascinating subject, you will find a list of highly recommended reading at the end of this book.

Over the years we have personally read all of the books that we recommend to you in order to support us both to rediscover our own health and wellness. The message is always the same. We have a choice every second of our lives to choose health and wellness. Simply by working in total harmony with our body and heart, ensuring that we always do what makes our hearts sing, is one sure-fire way of creating our own health and wellness. While this simple, but fundamental, message rings through all of the books, please do not miss the wonderful opportunity to read these authors' words, which could also change your life.

YOUR JOURNEY SO FAR:

- Your biography is not your destiny.
- You are free to make choices.
- Your health and wellness are affected by the choices you make; therefore it is important to be consciously aware of the choices you make, and to put these choices into perspective.
- The limiting beliefs you have about yourself are not true.
- You are an energetic being.
- Everything around you is made of energy.
- The physical matter that you perceive to be around you on a daily basis is merely energy vibrating at different speeds.
- Your thoughts change your brain and affect the chemical composition of your body on a second by second basis.
- As a result of this, your energetic frequency attracts towards it circumstances and people who resonate with your exact frequency.
- We manifest in our lives what we choose to think and feel – energy follows attention.
- The state of mindfulness follows attention. Being mindful allows you to change your perspective of the world; you take the pressure off yourself and begin to allow yourself to live healthfully and happily.
- The chakras and aura show your physical and energetic health. Be mindful of your own thoughts and the external influences that can affect these, in both positive and negative ways, as they affect your health and wellness.
- Your instinct is real and guides you safely through life.
- The ancients taught that we are so much more than our physical experience.
- You are part of everyone and everything; within you lies the reflection of the entire universe, and therefore consciousness and its latent and infinite potential lies within you.
- Your body and heart are always talking to you; listen in and take action to support your wellness.
- Tune into your heart and always run choices through it.

Just as nature flows; so do I.

STEP STONE TEN

MANAGING RESISTANCE

'Change is the essence of life. Be willing to surrender what you are for what you could become.'

Author unknown

At this point on your journey, the world around you may look slightly different. You have taken a gentle journey across some stepping stones, integrating ancient understanding and modern techniques into your daily life, helping you to rediscover and reconnect to your own potential for health and wellness.

For some of you, learning about yourself and coming face to face with the keys to your disharmony can seem like too high a hurdle to move beyond. It is very common for people to stay at this point on the journey for a while.

Perhaps you have identified that it is a partnership that is causing you to feel out of balance, or you simply know in your heart that you should leave your job because it isn't fulfilling you.

Remember that there is absolutely no judgement to be apportioned at this stage on your journey; you are right where you need to be. So, if you feel you need to wait for a while before you make any decisions, then this is exactly what you need to do. Let's put this into perspective.

🌿 If sitting and waiting a while helps you to regain harmony and peace, this is a clear choice, made from the heart, because perhaps you are not ready. Release any thoughts about 'shoulds' and 'oughts' because if your body is truly happy waiting a while, moving forward will not create harmony within your world, and more importantly, you are not listening to your body.

🍂 However, if sitting and waiting a while before you move forward creates negative feelings, this is a choice made from fear and your body is clearly asking you to move forward. Your ego, however, is telling you to stick with the familiar, but this is not creating health and wellness for you.

So, what do we do when we know that it is our fear-based ego that is affecting our decision to move forward and reconnect to health and wellness?

Any changes will affect not just us, but the important people within our world, as we know it at this particular moment. As we learn more about ourselves, and clear our energy field, letting go of stuck energy and negativity that has been part of us for eons, we may find that our relationships with others and our environment changes; this is a natural result of working on yourself. Perhaps your partner notices that you have been acting differently of late, or you find that the people you used to associate with no longer resonate with you and you find it difficult being in the same room as them.

We know that change is possible; it is a mere choice away. We also know that our ego protects us to keep us in the status quo; often at the detriment of our health and wellness. What if we make the 'wrong' choice? Understand that there is no such thing as a 'wrong' choice; it is just a choice that we make on our journey to enable us to move from point A to point B.

We, therefore, have two simple choices; one leads to wellness, the other to dis-ease, but some of us need to reach a tipping point to force our hand.

Often change does not occur if is overshadowed by our deepest fears such as our security, our protection or our standing in society. However, if our need to change from the heart is greater than our deepest fears, then change is inevitable, and we instantly choose the love response.

The tipping point for us came as a result of our fear-based egos letting go. Serious emotional and physical health conditions forced us to quit doing what we knew we should have stopped years ago. However, we would advise you never to find yourself in a situation such as that.

We resist out of old patterns and old habits. We know that change is not easy, but how many of us even allow ourselves to simply explore what living on the other side of a decision might look like?

By working in harmony with all parts of ourselves; including our ego, mind, body and heart, we give each of them a chance to tell their story. What might your world look like if you made a decision that was in harmony with all parts of yourself; that made your heart sing?

ACTIVITY

EXPLORATION - GIVING YOURSELF PERMISSION

This exercise has been adapted from NLP, known as time-line work. Within this exercise you can try out how it would feel to be older, looking back at the decisions you made (or didn't make) in life.

1. Make some space around you; enough to move around.

2. Now think about something within your world that you know you want to change but that you are resisting. Bring it clearly to mind; feel, see, sense, hear and taste everything associated with it.

3. Imagine a golden time-line moving out in front of you and behind you. In front of you on your time-line lies the rest of your life, behind you, the life that you have lived to date.

4. Bring your situation at this stage of your time-line back into focus in your mind. Imagine yourself doing nothing at all, simply continuing with the same thoughts, feelings, fears and anxieties associated with this.

5. When you are ready, open your eyes, step off your time-line, and go about five years into the future. Step back onto your time-line in the future, looking back at the 'you' in the present. How do you feel knowing that nothing has changed? What sensations do you have in your body?

6. Now, when you are ready, step off your time-line and move to the part of the time-line that represents the end of your life. Face the 'you' back in the present.

How do you now feel knowing that still nothing has changed? What sensations are you experiencing in your body?

7. Step off the time-line, and move slowly towards the present day. When you are ready, step back onto your time-line, facing your future, remembering how your life was when you left everything exactly as it was.

8. Now, bring the same situation at this stage of your time-line back into focus in your mind. Allow yourself to change this situation, doing exactly what it is that you would like to do in order to change your world, choosing to create the world around you from the heart, bringing peace and harmony into your world. Allow the image to change around you as you continue to stand on the time-line. Get a sense of how you feel; what is going on in your body. How does it feel? Where do you feel it? Is the sensation different?

9. When you are ready, open your eyes, step off your time-line and move about five years into the future. Step back onto your time-line in the future, looking back at the 'you' in the present. How do you now feel knowing that you changed your world, that you chose differently? What sensations do you now have in your body?

10. Step off your time-line again, and move to the end of your life. Step onto the time-line and face the 'you' in your present. How do you feel knowing that you changed your world? How is your world at the end of your life different to how it was when you didn't do anything? Experience every sensation; feel, hear, see, sense everything. Make a mental note of exactly what is happening for you.

11. Finally, when you are ready, step back off your time-line and slowly walk back to your present. Step back onto the time-line and bring into your conscious awareness how you felt with the two scenarios that you gave yourself permission to experience. Which one in particular brought you closer to health and wellness? Do you feel in a better position to make a decision having allowed yourself to explore the possibility?

In the exercise on the previous page you have simply given yourself permission to experience two different futures. It is a powerful exercise to allow the ego to try out how its world may appear as a result of separate decisions. It is especially helpful in bringing synergy to mind, body and soul and facilitating action.

While any journey of self-development takes time, and changes may not occur overnight, what no one can ever take away from you, once you have possession of them, are the basic teachings in this book. My (Louise) journey from ill-health, agoraphobia and depression to health and wellness took several years, and I am still a work in progress; incorporating these philosophies deeper and deeper into my world on a daily basis.

Any learnt skill takes time to become familiar and automatic. Do you remember your first driving lessons? Consciously thinking about when exactly to lift the accelerator pedal while pressing the clutch in, but over time these actions become second nature, filtering down into the subconscious until you have to consciously pull this information out into your conscious awareness in order to explain the process to someone (unless you are a driving instructor of course!).

What I also found particularly helpful, when I was travelling this path, was allowing myself to create a picture of my health condition, providing me with something tangible to focus on to help cut through any resistance that I may have felt.

ACTIVITY

LET'S GET CREATIVE

Get some big pieces of paper, multi-coloured pens and really go for it; be as expressive and creative as you wish. Once complete, meditate on your drawings in order to provide you with visual motivation to continue on your path.

Draw a picture of your issue – your illness, the situation you would like to change.

Draw a picture of what it would be like to be free of your issue – being well, being free.

Draw a picture of how you got there.

If we take the pressure off ourselves and realise that everything is merely an experience, that life simply is and that we can try out different experiences before we take physical action, we can gently nurture the ego, helping it to release its grip. As a result, we can commit to choosing the best experience we can.

YOUR JOURNEY SO FAR:

- Your biography is not your destiny.
- You are free to make choices.
- Your health and wellness are affected by the choices you make; therefore it is important to be consciously aware of the choices you make, and to put these choices into perspective.
- The limiting beliefs you have about yourself are not true.
- You are an energetic being.
- Everything around you is made of energy.
- The physical matter that you perceive to be around you on a daily basis is merely energy vibrating at different speeds.
- Your thoughts change your brain and affect the chemical composition of your body on a second by second basis.
- As a result of this, your energetic frequency attracts towards it circumstances and people who resonate with your exact frequency.
- We manifest in our lives what we choose to think and feel – energy follows attention.
- The state of mindfulness follows attention. Being mindful allows you to change your perspective of the world; you take the pressure off yourself and begin to allow yourself to live healthfully and happily.
- The chakras and aura show your physical and energetic health. Be mindful of your own thoughts and the external influences that can affect these, in both positive and negative ways, as they affect your health and wellness.
- Your instinct is real and guides you safely through life.
- The ancients taught that we are so much more than our physical experience.
- You are part of everyone and everything; within you lies the reflection of the entire universe, and therefore consciousness and its latent and infinite potential lies within you.
- Your body and heart are always talking to you; listen in and take action to support your wellness.
- Tune into your heart and always run choices through it.
- Resistance is futile and eventually leads to disharmony; allow yourself to explore possible futures.

By accepting the gifts of the universe
with love and gratitude in my heart,
I free myself to be magnificent.

'True love does not always give the receiver what it would like to receive, but it will always give that which is best for it. So welcome everything you receive whether you like it or not.

Ponder on anything you do not like, and see if you can see why it was necessary. Acceptance will then be very much easier.'

David Icke

Acceptance and gratitude are sub-emotions of love and are the actions that guide us ever closer to perfect health and wellness.

Acceptance

The term acceptance does not mean acquiescence; merely knowing when you can change a situation and when you can't. By now you should understand that the flow of life cannot be resisted. It is simply how we react to the flow of life that creates the world that we perceive to be around us. When we do this, we let go, yet know fundamentally that we all have a choice about how we react when life throws a challenging situation our way.

Acceptance follows on from resistance. When we know that our choice to resist is keeping us in the same situation, which is creating disharmony in our lives, we are not in a place to connect to health and wellness. The only way forward from resistance is to move into acceptance; accepting from the heart that which comes our way, in the same way that the droplet of water doesn't resist its pathway through gentle streams or raging torrents on its journey to the sea.

If we now look at Jason's experiences with bullying within the workplace, two issues of acceptance emerge from this story. The first is acceptance of the situation from the ego-state. Jason accepted the bullying for many years and resigned himself to the status quo. He accepted that while he couldn't change what was happening about the bullying, he convinced himself that everything else about his job was satisfactory. He told himself that it was far more important to remain in a job that he didn't like and in which he was experiencing high levels of stress because if he stayed he could continue to pay his household bills. Ultimately, change did not occur because Jason's ego kept him in a place where he believed he needed to pay the mortgage; at the time, the alternative seemed too difficult and scary to contemplate. When Jason ultimately began suffering with his health, as a result of the situation at work, he found himself in a position of acceptance because the ego had let go. He finally listened to his body, and with the ego exhausted, he took the decision from his heart to leave his job.

We know that the road of acceptance might not be easy. However, if we truly know in our heart the direction that we need to choose in order to preserve our health and wellness, then accepting what we know to be true in that moment, will save a great deal of unnecessary heartache in the future.

Gratitude

Thankfulness or appreciation is a positive emotion or attitude in acknowledgement of a benefit received. As we are all energetic beings, when we are in a sincere state of love or gratitude our vibrational signature (or resonance) is one of acceptance and harmony. As a result of this, our energy is vibrating at a higher frequency attracting towards us more experiences that are similar. This energetic signature also creates harmony within your energy field, leading on to health and wellness, because from this state you can let go. When we express gratitude and love for everything in our life – even those experiences that we might label 'bad' – we move into a harmonious, vibrational resonance, which attracts similar energies our way.

REFLECT

Think for a moment about a situation that you did not resonate with, that you might label 'bad'. There are two ways you can react:

1. From a place of love and gratitude – accepting that what happened, happened. As we know, anything that creates harmony within our body and mind maintains our health and wellness.

2. From a place of fear – why did that happen to me? What did I do wrong? You can probably think of more questions to ask, but how is this response helping you? How are you benefiting from feeling this way?

There are no winners or losers in anything. The only way to maintain peace and harmony within your body and mind is through choosing loving actions. Gratitude is one of these actions.

We spend our life giving labels to everything; this was a good experience, that one was bad, right or wrong. Yet these labels are merely formed by our own cultural references, environment and programming. One person might view a particular event as good, another as bad, depending on their view point and how they were affected.

Put simply, there is no such thing as right or wrong, good or bad. When we label experiences in this way, we begin to judge, and thereby create associated feelings within our body, which have a direct effect on our health and wellness. Without labels, we immediately take the pressure off ourselves. A droplet of water that streams out of the shower doesn't label its experience as good or bad; it simply 'is'. It follows the course of the water over your body, down into the plughole, into the drainage system and into the water treatment works, where it gets pumped back out into the mains water system to be used in someone's cup of tea, moving with the perfect ebb and flow of life.

Another droplet of water may be having a totally different experience, being gently evaporated out of the ocean into a cloud high in the sky, travelling hundreds of miles to be dropped as rain onto beautiful mountains, then to spend millions of years being purified through layers of rock emerging as spring water from a sacred well.

Nature teaches us a great deal, and because everything is interconnected, the macrocosm always reflects the microcosm.

Learn to observe life as nature does. Become the conscious observer, being aware of what is taking place around you and within you, and committing to move with the ebb and flow of life. Committing to what makes your heart sing.

Being thankful for those things that happen in our lives, helps us to put things into perspective, and to lift ourselves beyond the mere physicality of life; helping us to understand that we are so much more than our physical experience, awakening our spirituality, which we are all connected to from our heart centre. It helps us to become more positive about life, moving us out of our unbalanced egos and cultivating joy and happiness in our daily lives.

Ultimately, gratitude is a spiritual experience leading you into deeper layers of personal understanding and allowing you to let go.

Letting go

In our modern day culture, why do we try to control everything? Why do a large majority of the population suffer with anxiety, worry or anger? Why do many people experience insomnia?

The answer is that most of us have never really learnt how to let go, how to surrender. Just as we breathe in, we have to breathe out, because if we do not allow our body to continue this automotive response we die. At the end of our day we have to let go of the waking state in order to fall asleep to rejuvenate the body. Letting go is a natural and necessary part of life. In order to let go we must trust; we trust that our body's automotive breathing response will continue, yet we find it difficult to trust everything else within our lives and thereby create unnecessary resistance.

We must, however, only surrender to what feels right. There is no right or wrong – when you are connected, you will always choose the best way. Just stay in the flow, exactly like the water droplet on its journey to the sea.

To illustrate this point, we would like to share with you a well-known fable about a king and his master; King Janaka and Master Ashtavakra. One day, the king begged his spiritual teacher Ashtavakra to liberate him from illusion. Ashtavakra agreed, and the request was forgotten. Several days later, the king had forgotten all about his request when he heard a loud voice shouting for help from somewhere deep within the palace. Janaka recognised the voice as his beloved spiritual teacher Ashtavakra, and ran to his side only to find him screaming with both of his arms wrapped around a marble pillar, clinging on with all of his strength. Ashtavakra was screaming; 'Free me, free me! I am bound to this pillar, please help me, please!' The king was visibly distressed and looked at his master who seemed to have lost his mind. With tears in his eyes and shaking voice he said, 'Oh revered Master, what has happened to you? I can't see any ropes binding you to this pillar, nor is anyone holding you. Why don't you let go?' Ashtavakra shouted, 'You fool! Can you not see that I am bound? Liberate me please, set me free!' 'But Master,' the king stammered, 'nothing is holding you. Let go of the pillar and you will be free.'

At that moment, Ashtavakra calmly let go of the pillar and, standing free in front of his student said, 'You might feel that my behaviour was strange and absurd. But was it any more absurd than you asking me for liberation, when you are already and eternally free? Who is keeping you bound except for yourself?'

Many people find themselves in a relationship, a job, or a situation that they know has run its course and is no longer working, yet how many of them stay where they no longer feel comfortable? How many people do you know who have stayed for many years in a situation that makes them feel uncomfortable and unhappy? These dense frequencies of unhappiness course through the body, causing energetic imbalance, and if left unchecked, over time may cause physical and emotional illness.

What we need to realise is that we are keeping ourselves bound to those outdated situations; we simply make a choice to change our world if we decide to. As we found, our bodies couldn't take it any more, breaking down and leaving us with emotional and physical illness, which forced us to change our situations. However, if we had just listened earlier, we could have avoided unnecessary stress and upset, surrendering to the inevitability of the situation, following our heart's true desire.

Generally speaking, it is our ego that lies in the way of letting go. It is well documented that it is often easier to let go and surrender when we are exhausted, in despair, or when we have reached a dead end. In these cases, our ego is weakened and we finally admit that a change needs to be made. This is when we let go, surrendering to the natural ebb and flow of the universe.

It is not weak to let go; in fact, it is quite the opposite. It is empowering to let go, to understand that this simple act alone can help you to remain in your natural state of wellness, doing what it is that makes your heart sing. Why on earth waste energy worrying about those things that we cannot control, influence or change?

Anything that is out of alignment or resonance with your highest good, your joy and your happiness, needs to be examined.

'When I look back on all these worries I remember the story
of the old man who said on his deathbed that he had a
lot of trouble in his life, most of which had never happened.'

Winston Churchill

YOUR JOURNEY SO FAR:

- Your biography is not your destiny.
- You are free to make choices.
- Your health and wellness are affected by the choices you make; therefore it is important to be consciously aware of the choices you make, and to put these choices into perspective.
- The limiting beliefs you have about yourself are not true.
- You are an energetic being.
- Everything around you is made of energy.
- The physical matter that you perceive to be around you on a daily basis is merely energy vibrating at different speeds.
- Your thoughts change your brain and affect the chemical composition of your body on a second by second basis.
- As a result of this, your energetic frequency attracts towards it circumstances and people who resonate with your exact frequency.
- We manifest in our lives what we choose to think and feel – energy follows attention.
- The state of mindfulness follows attention. Being mindful allows you to change your perspective of the world; you take the pressure off yourself and begin to allow yourself to live healthfully and happily.
- The chakras and aura show your physical and energetic health. Be mindful of your own thoughts and the external influences that can affect these, in both positive and negative ways, as they affect your health and wellness.
- Your instinct is real and guides you safely through life.
- The ancients taught that we are so much more than our physical experience.
- You are part of everyone and everything; within you lies the reflection of the entire universe, and therefore consciousness and its latent and infinite potential lies within you.
- Your body and heart are always talking to you; listen in and take action to support your wellness.
- Tune into your heart and always run choices through it.
- Resistance is futile and eventually leads to disharmony; allow yourself to explore possible futures.
- Introduce acceptance and gratitude into your daily experience, committing to let go of anything that you cannot influence or change. Take the pressure off yourself.

Everything is perfect and exactly as it should be.

'Do you really want to look back on your life and see how wonderful it could have been had you not been afraid to live it?'

Dr Caroline Myss

After exploring acceptance, gratitude and letting go, we now move into another concept that states 'everything is perfect and exactly as it should be'. We move through life having specific expectations as to how things are going to be, or turn out, yet things rarely turn out exactly the way we expected because the universe is creating a bigger picture around us, one which we cannot see until we look back with the benefit of hindsight.

In order to take the pressure off yourself, from moment to moment within your life, and move ever closer to health and wellness, try to release any connection to expectations or outcomes. At the heart of many ancient cultures is the understanding that whatever will be, will be, and that you are exactly where you are supposed to be at that moment in time, even though you might not understand why that is. The ancients viewed situations as they were, not as they wanted them to be.

One day, a king was in his kitchen, playing with a very sharp knife. As he threw it up into the air, the knife span awkwardly, spiralling down at a great speed towards the king's fingers. Within a split second, the knife sliced cleanly through two of the king's fingers, removing them at the knuckle. The king became extremely distressed, shouting to his spiritual minister for comfort and support. However, the minister merely looked at the king and gently said 'That happened for your highest good'. The king flew into a rage, and ordered his minister to be locked up in the palace dungeons. Furious, the king then rode at breakneck speed into the forest in a bid to clear his mind and regain some composure.

After a while, the king realised that he had strayed from the path and he was deep in an unknown part of the forest. Hearing a rustling of vegetation in front of him, he stopped his trusty steed and watched as a group of tribespeople appeared in front of him. Shouting in an unknown language, they surrounded the king and took him to their chief. The king realised that they were cannibals and were probably going to eat him. However, as the cannibals inspected their future dinner more closely, they animatedly pointed to his missing fingers. The cannibals were unable to eat their 'prize' if it was not perfect in every way.

The king was set free and he rode back to his palace with joy and happiness in his heart, ecstatic at his freedom. When he arrived at the palace, he ran down to the dungeons immediately, and threw himself at his master's feet. 'Master, I am so sorry,' cried the king and shared his story about being saved from the jaws of certain death because he had lost two fingers, 'How can you ever forgive me for locking you in the dungeon?'. His master smiled, and said 'Beloved king, it was for my highest good. Please don't be so upset'. 'But how can you say that?' said the king incredulously. 'Dearest king, if you hadn't locked me in the dungeon yesterday then I would have ridden out with you into the forest. As you were imperfect, the cannibals would have eaten me instead!'

What we realise through this fable is that we cannot really know what is best for us, because we do not see the bigger picture. By allowing what is to simply be, we become free to either change, or leave things, without losing peace of mind.

YOUR JOURNEY SO FAR:

- Your biography is not your destiny.
- You are free to make choices.
- Your health and wellness are affected by the choices you make; therefore it is important to be consciously aware of the choices you make, and to put these choices into perspective.
- The limiting beliefs you have about yourself are not true.
- You are an energetic being.
- Everything around you is made of energy.
- The physical matter that you perceive to be around you on a daily basis is merely energy vibrating at different speeds.
- Your thoughts change your brain and affect the chemical composition of your body on a second by second basis.
- As a result of this, your energetic frequency attracts towards it circumstances and people who resonate with your exact frequency.
- We manifest in our lives what we choose to think and feel – energy follows attention.
- The state of mindfulness follows attention. Being mindful allows you to change your perspective of the world; you take the pressure off yourself and begin to allow yourself to live healthfully and happily.
- The chakras and aura show your physical and energetic health. Be mindful of your own thoughts and the external influences that can affect these, in both positive and negative ways, as they affect your health and wellness.
- Your instinct is real and guides you safely through life.
- The ancients taught that we are so much more than our physical experience.
- You are part of everyone and everything; within you lies the reflection of the entire universe, and therefore consciousness and its latent and infinite potential lies within you.
- Your body and heart are always talking to you; listen in and take action to support your wellness.
- Tune into your heart and always run choices through it.
- Resistance is futile and eventually leads to disharmony; allow yourself to explore possible futures.
- Introduce acceptance and gratitude into your daily experience, committing to let go of anything that you cannot influence or change. Take the pressure off yourself.
- Everything is perfect; we do not know the bigger picture so allow yourself to 'be'.
- Release expectations about the outcome of events – the universe paints a better picture than we ever could.

I possess all the strength and dedication I need to reconnect to health and wellness.

'No one outside ourselves can rule us inwardly. When we know this, we become free.'

Buddha

In order to achieve the most from this book and your development, it is important that you commit seriously to the following.

1. Be the best you, you can be. Identify your limiting beliefs and commit to dissolving them. They are simply not true. Choose love, not fear.

2. Take responsibility for the choices you make; no one is to blame.

3. Practise non-judgement, love, compassion and respect for all, including yourself. When you do this, you automatically create a positive vibration around you leading to health and wellness. Why waste energy casting aspersions or judgement on others, when you are not them and cannot see their view of the world?

4. Be grateful for what you have got, instead of focusing on what you haven't got. When you do this, you create more abundance in your life, as a result of focusing on it, no matter how small.

5. Be truthful and speak your truth with love. Stand up and be the person you truly are, not the one that you feel you should show to the world. It is time to be the real you, aligning your body and soul to peace and harmony.

6. Live your truth authentically and with integrity. When you live this way, your energy signature radiates out to others that you are confident in your own skin and they respond accordingly. Speak freely, yet thoughtfully from the heart.

7. Be humble. Understand that everyone has a message and a story to tell, which is equally as important as everyone else's – there is no one any better or worse than you. We are each a part of each other, and as a result are totally connected.

8. Ask, how can I serve? We are each in service to each other. Working through the heart and committing to our own reconnection to health and wellness, we not only support ourselves, but everyone around us. Everyone gains.

9. Commit to working through your stuff. Life is a work in progress, have fun on the way.

10. Give yourself permission to be yourself – even if it means changing; know that the universe will support you.

Perhaps you could transcribe these points onto a piece of paper and pin it up where you will see it on a daily basis.

**My body is my vehicle for this incarnation;
what I internalise, I become.**

STEP STONE FOURTEEN

CLEARING THE BODY PHYSICALLY

'Take only what you need
and leave the rest.
      Use the world; don't abuse it.'

Toltec wisdom

As Dr Bruce Lipton identified in his research, there are three causes for disruption in the healthy signalling of the body:

- Trauma: accidents cause a disruption in the brain signal.
- Toxins interfere with the body's signalling chemistry.
- The mind: if the mind sends inappropriate signals at the wrong times, our systems become imbalanced and diseased.

Throughout this book, we have focused on techniques to support your new view of the world. Now we would like to focus on the issue of toxins and how they can affect the natural chemistry of the body. This imbalance can also affect the delicate energy system of the body, the functioning of the chakras and the aura.

A toxin is generally described as something that is poisonous and harmful to the body. When we talk about toxins in this context, we are referring to the toxins that can be found in medication, personal products, cleaning products, our environment and the food we eat, particularly meat filled with antibiotics, processed food and genetically modified food. Some foods are contaminated as a result of pesticides, herbicides or other chemicals. Food grown in the earth can sometimes be contaminated with heavy metals as a result of the composition of the surrounding soil.

The body is known to store toxins and common symptoms of toxicity within the body system can include headaches, fatigue, muscle pains, indigestion, constipation, dizziness and poor coordination.

While we are not suggesting that you take drastic action and change your diet completely, it is useful to consider what gentle changes you can begin to make to your lifestyle and become more aware of what you use within your body and externally.

- Consider a vegetarian or fish diet.
- Eat plenty of fresh fruit and vegetables, organic if possible.
- Drink enough fresh, spring water. Consider fitting a water filter.
- Reduce the amount of processed food in your diet.
- Cut down on your salt intake.
- Abstain from alcohol, cigarettes or any drugs (apart from regular medication under supervision from your GP).
- Try to cook all meals with fresh ingredients, preferably organic.
- Grow and cook your own vegetables (if space is a problem, grow things vertically such as beans, peas, peppers and sprouts, or grow vegetables in tubs for limited harvests). Always grow from organic seed. Give it a go; it's easier than you may think.
- Look at your personal care products. How many of them contain SLS (sodium lauryl sulphate) or parabens? All good health food shops now sell products free of parabens and SLS.
- Instead of cane sugar substitute natural alternatives including honey, agave syrup and fructose.
- Decrease the amount of tea and coffee you drink and substitute with hot water and lemon or herbal tea. If you really need tea and coffee, switch to non-stimulating, decaffeinated types.
- Research essential oils for cleaning your home; avoid using harsh chemicals or bleach within your environment.
- Get plenty of rest and sleep.
- Drink fruit juice diluted with water (pure juices are very high in sugar so ensure you protect your teeth as much as you can).

As a result of purifying our diet, we both experienced immediate beneficial changes within our overall wellness. We discovered we had far more energy. We would wake up and not feel 'sluggish', our skin tone and texture improved, our moods were far more balanced. We felt more positive, and best of all, we lost weight. We can only share with you, of course, what has worked for us, but suffice to say that the difference in our lives has been startling.

In the first instance, we would guide you to complete as much research as you can before you make any changes at all and always discuss your plans with your GP. You might also like to seek the advice of a good nutritionist; we have provided some useful contacts and resources at the end of this book.

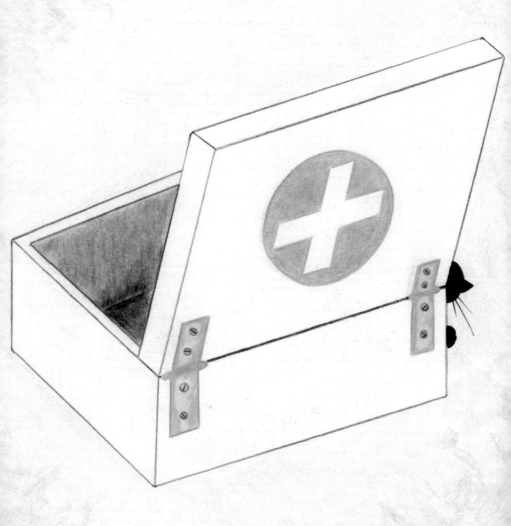

Everything I need is within me.

STEP STONE FIFTEEN

BASIC PRINCIPLES AND TOOLS TO INTEGRATE INTO DAILY LIFE

'There are two ways to live your life – one is as though nothing is a miracle, the other is as though everything is a miracle.'

Albert Einstein

It is well-known that people with a positive outlook, live calmer happier and healthier lives. Looking at life in a more mindful way, via the methods described in this book, can help you to reclaim health, serenity and wellness. What follows are some practical tools to support you along your journey.

Here are some useful questions to ask yourself, to help monitor your current state of wellness.

- How does it feel to you to surrender to the situation and accept what is happening?
- Does it make your heart sing? If the answer is no, do you really need it in your life? Doing something that you do not like will create an imbalance of energy within your energy field and, over time, could result in poor health.
- What benefit does it serve you?
- How can you change your state from fear, to one of peace, love and acceptance?

Breathing

Most people do not know how to breathe properly; they breathe too shallowly. Breathing correctly is the best way to ground and reconnect.

ACTIVITY

FOCUS THE BREATH

- Close your eyes and focus on your breath (fill all of your lungs, not just the top half).
- Visualise gold light 6in (15cm) above the top of your head.
- As you inhale, draw this light into the top of your head following a line down your spine to the base and onwards to your feet.
- As you exhale, visualise the light travelling back up your spine and out of the top of your head.
- Each breath should be deep and complete, taking the energy throughout the body.

Grounding

The grounding process puts you in contact with the Earth, as well as your own body, helping you to feel more 'present'. It is advisable to make grounding part of your daily routine.

ACTIVITY

GROUNDING

1. Visualise golden roots growing out of the soles of each of your feet, reaching through the soil and the rock, deep into the Earth. Waiting for you in the centre of the Earth is a beautiful crystal around which you can wrap your roots. Ensure you are fully anchored.

2. Envisage that your whole body is 'straightening' out physically, emotionally, mentally and physically.

3. Concentrate on your feet, visualise them surrounded by cool soil.

4. Hold a grounding crystal such as haematite, smoky quartz, black tourmaline or Jasper.

Protection

You would never go outside in the rain without an umbrella or a coat because you would get very wet indeed. The same principle applies to energy that you might not be able to see physically, but nevertheless is very real.

Every day when you leave your home you interact with other people and come into contact with their aura and their energy frequencies, as well as environmental pollution from mobile phones and TV masts.

Without being sufficiently protected or shielded this energy can stick to you, leaving you feeling tired, depressed, anxious, angry and a whole myriad of other emotions.

ACTIVITY

PROTECTION

1. Envisage a golden-white light showering down over your head from the cosmos, surrounding you in front, behind, to your right, your left, above you and below you. Surround your whole being and your aura in all directions.

2. Make this bubble of light as thick as you would like it to be, affirming that you are safe and protected on the inside of the bubble from anything that is not for your highest good.

3. For extra protection you can place mirrors on the outside of the bubble. Direct the mirrors into the Earth, reflecting anything that is unlike love and light into the Earth to be transmuted into love.

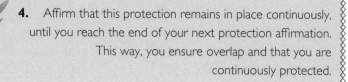

4. Affirm that this protection remains in place continuously, until you reach the end of your next protection affirmation. This way, you ensure overlap and that you are continuously protected.

Auric clearing

Protecting yourself and your aura every day is essential to limit energetic debris.

Crystals

Crystals are excellent at cleansing, protecting and grounding. Choose a crystal that you feel drawn to, using your intuition. Dedicate it to the highest good by saying something like 'I dedicate this crystal to the highest and purest energy', then place the crystal where you need it or put it in your pocket and carry it around with you for peace of mind.

- Grounding crystals: haematite, red jasper, black tourmaline.
- Protective crystals: smoky quartz, black tourmaline, haematite.
- Peace-giving crystals: green calcite, rose quartz, blue calcite, clear quartz.

Affirmations and positive thinking

Affirmations are fabulous to reinforce positive beliefs about yourself and are very helpful in negating limiting beliefs. Try saying these affirmations to yourself for 5 to 10 minutes several times each day. Remember that energy follows intention/attention, so that over time you will feel your affirmations and you will become your affirmations.

1. I AM perfect exactly the way I am.

2. I AM happy, healthy, safe and protected.

3. I AM in perfect health and wellness.

4. I AM positive in everything I say, think and do.

5. I AM peaceful and calm.

6. I release everything that is holding me back.

7. My world is filled with love, joy, beauty, peace and comfort, always.

8. I AM perfectly guided; I love life and life loves me.

9. I choose to think only positive thoughts.

10. I deserve love, happiness and abundance.

'Life moves pretty fast.
If you don't stop and look around once in a while, you could miss it.'
Ferris Bueller

I AM the perfect embodiment of health and wellness.

STEP STONE SIXTEEN

HOW WILL YOU KNOW IF YOU ARE MAKING POSITIVE CHANGES?

'The soul is placed in the body like a rough diamond, and must be polished, or the lustre of it will never appear.'

Daniel Defoe

What follows are just some of the ways that you may now be feeling, as a result of working through this book, throwing off your labels and reconnecting to your potential.

- Possession of a certain ability to go with the flow of life.
- Flexible and open to change.
- Not seeking to judge or control, knowing that life cannot be tamed.
- Possession of a renewed sense of humour, not taking yourself too seriously.
- An ability to let go of painful memories with love, forgiveness and gratitude.
- Feel neutral about things you used to be upset about.

Whatever your religion or belief system, life simply is, allow it to be. Follow the heart, commit to love and know that everything will be OK.

While you may, at times, feel that all hope is lost, or that you haven't made any progress at all, know that you have. Allow the emotions to come up, listen to what they want to say to you, then if you feel ready, thank them and let them go, with acceptance, gratitude and love. By doing this, you deal with emotions as they surface, ensuring that you do not stuff them back down, to cause you more problems in the future. You are simply a work in progress, so take the pressure off yourself.

It might surprise you to realise that we experienced many, what we perceived to be, 'set-backs' on our journey. Louise still had to visit hospital when her atrial fibrillation started, yet it was how she dealt with the condition when it happened that was the key. At the beginning of her journey, she reacted from a place of fear because she was depressed and suffered from severe anxiety, making the condition ten times worse. Over time, by genuinely integrating these teachings into her psyche and daily life, when she did experience an episode, she was able to remain calm and peaceful, knowing that everything was exactly as it was meant to be, trusting totally in the intelligence of the universe. Jason also used these teachings to gain confidence about his place in the world and stand up for himself from a place of love, developing a deep love and appreciation for life. Over time, we successfully reconnected to the love and peace at the centre of creation and now truly understand what it is like to genuinely rediscover our own health and wellness, free of labels and limiting beliefs.

ACTIVITY

REVIEW PROGRESS

Now is the time to bring your attention back to one of the first exercises in this book where you identified the limiting beliefs and labels you had about yourself. If you feel ready, take the sheet of paper out of its safe place.

Take a look at everything you wrote, reviewing it one last time. Do you recognise yourself? Are those labels or beliefs surprising to you now? How far do you think you have come on your journey?

Those labels were simply you in a snap-shot in time. Your biography is not your destiny and you can say goodbye to these, if you choose to. As a symbolic act you can choose to let go of that old part of you – shred the paper, burn it, or simply throw it away. Choose whatever feels right to you and reconnect to everything that you were never actually disconnected from.

Well done! The way is clear for you to be magnificent. The way is clear for you to achieve your full potential and maintain your daily health and wellness.

None of us on this planet stop learning, and each one of us is a work in progress until the day we die and beyond; but while travelling this journey why not consciously choose love and see just how much easier your life flows.

A SUMMARY OF
STEP STONE WISDOM

Choices: love or fear?

- Your biography is not your destiny.
- You are free to make choices.
- Your health and wellness are affected by the choices you make; therefore it is important to be consciously aware of the choices you make, and to put these choices into perspective.
- The limiting beliefs you have about yourself are not true.
- Being aware and putting your world into perspective is a vital pathway towards health and wellness.

The atom and vibration

- You are an energetic being.
- Everything around you is made of energy.
- The physical matter that you perceive to be around you on a daily basis is merely energy vibrating at different speeds.

Resonance

- Your thoughts change your brain and affect the chemical composition of your body on a second by second basis.
- As a result of this, your energetic frequency attracts towards it circumstances and people who resonate with your exact frequency.
- We manifest in our lives what we choose to think and feel – energy follows attention.

Mindfulness and shifting into NEUTRAL

- The state of mindfulness follows attention. Being mindful allows you to change your perspective of the world; you take the pressure off yourself and begin to allow yourself to live healthfully and happily.

Vibration: the aura, chakras and stress

🪷 The chakras and aura show your physical and energetic health. Be mindful of your own thoughts, and external influences that can affect these in both positive and negative ways, as they affect your health and wellness.

Your natural instinct

🪷 Your instinct is real and guides you safely through life.

🪷 The ancients taught that we are so much more than our physical experience.

🪷 You are part of everyone and everything; within you lies the reflection of the entire universe, and therefore consciousness and its latent and infinite potential lie within you.

Your body is talking; are you listening?

🪷 Your body and heart are always talking to you; listen in and take action to support your wellness.

🪷 Tune into your heart and always run choices through it.

Managing resistance

🪷 Resistance is futile and eventually leads to disharmony; allow yourself to explore possible futures.

Acceptance, gratitude and letting go

🪷 Introduce acceptance and gratitude into your daily experience, committing to let go of anything that you cannot influence or change. Take the pressure off yourself.

Everything is perfect

- Everything is perfect; we do not know the bigger picture so allow yourself to 'be'.
- Release expectations about the outcome of events – the universe paints a better picture than we ever could.

Clearing the body physically

- Identify toxins within your physical body that may be affecting your health and wellness and reflect on whether it feels appropriate to reduce them. (Always discuss any changes in medication or dietary changes with your GP first.)

Basic tools and principles

- Complete grounding, auric clearing and protection work every day.
- Maintain a healthy daily diet and nutrition.
- Drink enough fresh, pure water.
- Maintain a healthy routine – exercise, have a daily walk, get out into the elements.
- Practise regular quiet time, meditation, visualisation and contemplation.
- Get enough sleep.

EPILOGUE

Today I am well
Today I am at peace
Today I am in love with life and life loves me,
it nurtures me and supports me in everything I do.
I am truly blessed to be here and to have had the experiences in life that I have.
Thank you
With unconditional love from the Universal Heart
Blessed be

Louise and Jason

FURTHER READING AND
USEFUL CONTACTS

🪷 *The HeartMath Solution*, Doc Childre and Howard Martin. HarperCollins, New York, 199⁶

🪷 *I AM Here*, Sandy Stevenson. Weiser, York Beach ME, 2000.

🪷 *The Celestine Prophecy*, James Redfield. Bantam, London, 1994.

🪷 *How Your Mind Can Heal Your Body*, David Hamilton. Hay House, London, 2008.

🪷 *Why Kindness is Good For You*, David Hamilton. Hay House, London, 2010.

🪷 *Why People Don't Heal and How They Can*, Caroline Myss. Three Rivers Press, 1998.

🪷 *Beyond the Obvious,* Christine Page. Random House, London, 2004.

🪷 *The Wave,* Jude Currivan. O Books, London, 2005.

🪷 *The 13th Step*, Jude Currivan. Hay House, London, 2007.

🪷 *The 8th Chakra*, Jude Currivan. Hay House, London, 2006.

🪷 *CosMos*, Jude Currivan and Dr Ervin Laszlo. Hay House, London, 2008.

🪷 *The Biology of Belief,* Bruce Lipton. Mountain of Love, Santa Rosa – CA, 2005.

🪷 *You Can Heal Your Life*, Louise Hay. Hay House, London, 2005.

🪷 *The Crystal Bible*, Judy Hall. Godsfield Press, Hampshire, 2003.

Contacts

British Association for Counselling and Psychotherapy
BACP House
15 St John's Business Park
Lutterworth
LE17 4HB
www.bacp.co.uk
Tel: 01455 883300

Complementary Medical Association
www.the-cma.org.uk

DiscoverSerenity Holistic Solutions - Workshops, courses and therapies
www.discoverserenity.co.uk

Jason Paul Claire Artwork - Prints, original drawings/paintings, cards and bookmarks
www.discoverserenity.co.uk/intuitiveart.htm

MIND
www.mind.org.uk
Tel: 01455 550243

Nutrition Society
www.nutritionsociety.org

OUR NEXT BOOK

As we leave you to work on our next book, we wish to deepen the understanding we have shared with you by introducing an ancient concept – our outer world is an expression of our inner world.

By now you know that when we ignore the universe, we ignore what we need to know; what is actually right in front of our very eyes. When the universe is ignored, sometimes over many years, it tries more and more innovative ways to get us to pay attention, sometimes to the point of making us physically ill. This is why we must continue to listen and be aware of what is going on around us because, only when we do this, can we truly start to change what is happening. We must be aware and listen, and commit to change. If we do not, we repeat the same patterns. We can take a step back and become the writer of our own script, thereby changing the movie playing on our internal screen of life – what we refer to as 'the now'.

In the next book we will take you on a journey to meet your soul, through the eye of your heart. We look forward to seeing you there!"

> **The Oneness Code** – coming soon.

Keep up to date with progress at **www.discoverserenity.co.uk**